Teaching Pupils with Severe
and Complex Difficulties

of related interest

Incorporating Social Goals in the Classroom
A Guide for Teachers and Parents of Children
with High-Functioning Autism and Asperger Syndrome
Rebecca A. Moyes
Foreword by Susan J. Moreno
ISBN 1 85302 967 X

Behavioural Concerns and Autistic Spectrum Disorders
Explanations and Strategies for Change
John Clements and Ewa Zarkowska
ISBN 1 85302 742 1

Social Cognition Through Drama and Literature
for People with Learning Disabilities
Macbeth in Mind
Nicola Grove and Keith Park
ISBN 1 85302 908 4

Odyssey Now
Nicola Grove and Keith Park
ISBN 1 85302 315 9

People Skills for Young Adults
Marianna Csoti
ISBN 1 85302 716 2

Asperger's Syndrome
A Guide for Parents and Professionals
Tony Attwood
ISBN 1 85302 577 1

Enabling Communication in Children with Autism
Carol Potter and Chris Whittaker
ISBN 1 85302 956 4

Teaching Pupils with Severe and Complex Difficulties

Back to First Principles

Christopher Dyer

Jessica Kingsley Publishers
London and Philadelphia

First published in the United Kingdom in 2001 by
Jessica Kingsley Publishers Ltd
116 Pentonville Road
London N1 9JB, England
and
325 Chestnut Street
Philadelphia, PA 19106, USA

www.jkp.com

Library of Congress Cataloging in Publication Data
A CIP catalog record for this book is available from the Library of Congress

British Library Cataloguing in Publication Data
A CIP catalogue record for this book is available from the British Library

ISBN 1 85302 951 3

Printed and Bound in Great Britain by
Athenaeum Press, Gateshead, Tyne and Wear

Contents

ACKNOWLEDGEMENTS   8

1 Introduction   9

2 Principal Principles   18

3 Detective Stories   37

4 Language   58

5 Thinking   94

6 Behaviour   124

7 Endpiece   167

APPENDIX   172

BIBLIOGRAPHY   175

SUBJECT INDEX   181

AUTHOR INDEX   186

INDEX TO PRINCIPLES   188

To the memory of B. S. without whom…

Acknowledgements

While the notions put forward in this book, errors, omissions and shortcomings included, are alone my responsibility I am indebted to many people in the formulation of the ideas which follow.

A period of in-service staff education for the London Borough of Newham meant that I had the great advantage of frequent and searching discussions around some of the ideas within this book and for those I am grateful both to the teachers on courses and to colleagues: to Dorita Friend, who may well discover that I have, without meaning to, used her ideas at times as if my own; to Barbara Burke for challenges beyond number; to Judith Roux for refining my ideas on linguistics in the context of children set to learn in classrooms.

As part of the team discussing the most apt provision for pupils whose needs came to the point of Statements under the Law I had the honour of working with and learning from Dr Tom Ravenette and Ian Millward as successive and valued principal educational psychologist colleagues. The in-depth discussions that each pupil engendered gave the lie to those who assume that local education authorities (in England) simply 'rubber stamp' appropriate ways forward in meeting the needs of those with serious and complex learning difficulties.

An invitation to conduct seminars on severe learning difficulties in Moravia in the Czech Republic also served to sharpen ideas and widen contexts. In addition to those university students of exceptional language skills who interpreted for me and therefore gave me a voice, I also met many colleagues whose enthusiasms and thought processes were invigorating, of whom Květa Staňková, Etel Smekalová, Milena Tejklová and Pěva Zaludová deserve a mention.

My wife Angela has, over many years, lived with, suggested and discussed snatches of the ideas in this book, read the drafts, pointed out the inconsistencies and set me right on the difference between a spin drier and a tumble drier! My gratitude and thanks.

Finally, but above all, I owe respect and gratitude to the many children who, over the years of my professional life, have set before me their difficulties in learning and trusted me to try to help them. The dialogue that they offered to me has not, I hope, been betrayed in this book.

CHAPTER I

Introduction

The idea for this book arose out of work with teachers and other professionals that I undertook both in the London Borough of Newham and in Moravia, in the Czech Republic, between 1988 and 1997.

The immediate circumstance of the work in both locations was a call from professionals for some help in meeting the developing pressure from many quarters. There was, on the one hand, some perplexity for staff in being asked to receive into ordinary education pupils who were experiencing severe difficulties in learning and, on the other, for staff in special schools of finding a new vocabulary for reporting, to a new inspectorial system, what they had been doing for some time. For teachers in both places it was, at times, a reluctant but still a largely positive response to the impact that the worldwide movement for *inclusion* was making in educational thought.

Turning that *thought* into educational *practice* required some return to first principles. The more pupils appeared to deviate from the 'normal' expectations of classroom learning, the more anxious staff were that they, themselves, would not be able to use their trained, professional skills on behalf of pupils with more severe difficulties. A return to first principles, however, suggested that the basis of teaching and education remained constant, no matter what the difficulties of the pupils might be at first glance. I was fortunate, therefore, to have the opportunity to co-operate in devising courses and seminars and to participate in individual case-study discussions where professional colleagues were prepared to spend time considering the theoretical background of *why* children were affected in certain ways as a means of opening up understanding of *why* a particular individual pathway for a child might be considered, adapted or rejected.

Foundations

It is an unfortunate tendency in English educational circles – and it seems to me peculiarly *English* – that there has been a reluctance to consider the philosophical foundations and theoretical principles upon which profitable educational practice should be based. The call has been repeatedly for *programmes* for universal application in classrooms; for an answer to 'What must I do?' without asking the prior question 'Why must I do it?' Therefore such programmes and *methods* appear as answers to questions that might not apply to one or to any of the individual children subjected to them. This might have been seen to be the case had the relevant question been asked. The result is often sadly predictable: that the educational philosopher and the thinking teacher are reduced to attempting to explain why things went wrong, why standards were not being raised, rather than being encouraged, and indeed required, to set out the underlying principles upon which education should move towards the goal of betterment for all.

When discussion with teachers starts from the perspective of thinking about the underlying principles and focuses from this standpoint upon specific aspects of the educational process, then it appears that the staff begin to realise that they have, indeed, the skills and insights to meet a whole variety of needs and that they understand their children the better.

Once that is realised, any programmes and procedures can be critically evaluated in relation to individual children. They are then carried out to a purpose and not simply carried out against a tick-list. The tick-list is an all too common substitute for real educational outcomes for a child. This book is not seeking to deny the place of ordered schemes for teaching pupils. Planning for stated objectives is a foundation of good teaching and a means of evaluating its outcomes. Special education has had a long history of developing precise learning targets and progress charts. Nevertheless, education for all children, but perhaps especially for those in most difficulty, has to take account of the paramount need to focus upon and to trigger the *learning potential* of each individual child. The child is not to be categorised under medical or psychological syndromes, although known characteristics of such syndromes need to be understood for the manner in which they affect functional learning in general. Each child, however, will present with individual differences and it is the individual differences that need to be understood before programmes are drawn up.

For that reason this book does not seek to give detailed guidance on how to approach any particular syndrome of learning difficulty; although, where necessary, reference to particular identifiable characteristics of a relevant condition may be made along the way. Rather it will seek to go back to *principles*[1] that hold universally for all children; then offer some *implications* of each principle as an aid to the planning of Individual Education Programmes (IEPs) as applied to those children with the severest difficulties in learning. In this way it will seek to free experienced teachers to apply what is written here by using their own accumulated expertise when deciding upon tactics that might be usefully employed for any individual pupil, taken, as judged appropriate, from any or none of the published programmes that they might come across. It will also seek to offer to students, in initial teacher training, reference points against which they can begin to evaluate their introduction to meeting special educational needs.

Concerning principles

The discussion that follows starts with a consideration of the *principal principles*: those essential precursors to educated growth that every child needs and, indeed, most acquire in the natural course of their early life. It is the misfortune of those children with the greatest difficulty that often they do not *experience* these aspects of growth or experience them imperfectly. Such principles, therefore, are not exclusive to pupils with severe difficulties and, indeed, need addressing in any educational approach. The difference is that for pupils with learning difficulties they cannot simply be taken for granted as having happened in the normal course of development. Such principles need to underpin both curriculum planning in the broad view and classroom practice in the particular view to ensure the effective educational advance of each pupil.

Experience defined

A word, at this point, about what I mean here by 'experience'. Throughout this book it is taken to mean that a pupil has been able to bring an event into the conscious brain; to recognise it as something in which he or she has taken part. The event, therefore, has some *meaning*. For the purpose of this definition it is irrelevant whether the meaning that the event has for a particular child is shared by another: a child can have a purely idiosyncratic experience. Education and social interaction, generally in the course of growth, come to modify the potential for *shared* meaning: provided the child is conscious of having experienced something – whatever it may be. For some children with severe difficulties, however, it is as if what happens to them during some stages of their development does not directly register in such a way. 'Experience', in the sense used here, is not a physical entity (although generally speaking one has to be there corporeally) but rather an *internalising process*. For a child to experience something she or he has to have the capacity to:

- be aware that there is an occurrence
- seek to find a meaning within it
- be able to store that meaning for future expansion.

In awareness, in its turn, it is not sufficient for her or for him merely to have a body contiguous to the occurrence. The important thing is that an active part of the mind is also engaged.

As an example of what I mean, let us take a train journey through the Channel Tunnel from England to France. Let us assume that I board the train in Waterloo Station, London (England) and fall asleep in my seat before reaching the tunnel entrance in Kent. I next wake from my slumbers as the train is entering the suburbs of Paris. The evidence that I have travelled through the tunnel is clear. I am within the borders of the city of Paris (France), I am in the same seat of the same carriage as at Waterloo, and my companion is the same person and assures me that the train did, indeed, go under the English Channel. But I have not *experienced* the Channel Tunnel. I can tell you nothing about it nor about any impression I might have gained underground, even if only of outside darkness. There is nothing to stick in my memory. For my tunnel transit to register it would have needed my companion to dig me in the ribs as we entered it and thus bring the tunnel experience into my conscious mind.

This 'digging in the ribs' is an apt metaphor for the role of the teacher in bringing what is happening into the conscious experience of a pupil. It is not fanciful to say that many pupils with the profoundest difficulties may have reached formal education without having experienced many of the situations through which they have passed; or may have experienced them spasmodically and so have formed an apparently strange and disjointed view of what life is about.

The importance of imagination

In studying how to ensure that pupils are in a position to experience the teaching on offer the teacher's main effective weapon is *imagination*. Imagination, the power to imagine ourselves into situations beyond our own actual experience by reference to our store of memory of the experiences we have had, allows us to make calculated assumptions about what it must be like to be another person in another circumstance. Teachers can, therefore, use clues gained from observation to imagine themselves into the particular circumstances of particular children. Of course none of us can *know* what it is like to operate with another person's brain but we make daily adjustments on the basis of what we assume is a common thread of human thoughts and feelings. When, however, we may need to make the effort to think ourselves into the thought process of a pupil with severe difficulties, we must have recourse to more than we have directly experienced. We need to use our imagination.

INSIDE OUT

For this we must work *from the inside out* – from a reasoned imagination of what might be happening in the inside of a pupil's mind as a precursor to an attempted explanation of what is manifest in the behaviours noticeable on the outside.

The observational approach that enables teachers to establish the clues upon which to let the imagination play is the subject of Chapter 3, 'Detective Stories'.

The appropriateness of this title was brought home to me by a student of psychology from the University of Brno in the Czech Republic. She had been interpreting for me when I was asked to work with a child with complex difficulties, his parents and the professionals involved with him. In the car, on the way back from an outlying country district to the city of Olomouc, she talked about how the difficulties the child faced, *from the inside*, began to unravel both in the questions I had asked during observation and from the subsequent discussion, and said: 'It was fascinating how the clues came together – just like a detective story.' The analogy, I felt, was apt. A truly individual educational approach is only possible as a result of careful detective work to determine, on his or her behalf, how each particular pupil functions; it goes beyond what the medical diagnosis or psychological assessment might be. As in all good detective stories, the 'forensic' opinion (by which, in this case I mean the tests both medical and psychological) carries a lot of weight but, by itself, it does not solve the central problem. It needs the skill and flair of the detective to draw it all together.

Language and thinking

The next two chapters concentrate on *language* and *thinking*. Strictly, to accord with the most recent ideas, thinking should precede language. There is clear evidence emerging that a baby's thinking mechanism is in place before language develops the means to express and rationalise the thoughts (Nelson 1996); but then again, there is evidence that language is instinctive (Pinker 1994) and is also in place before it develops the sophistication to demonstrate that thinking is in place! The two mechanisms are so intertwined as to be virtually inseparable. Language is put first if only because the ability to *speak* is often regarded as the most potent distinguishing mark in children with severe difficulties. Being able to speak, as will be argued, is not the same as possessing useful linguistic capability. Nevertheless it remains a powerful indicator of human bonding and of the normality that most parents (and other adults) look for, asking, 'Will my child be able to speak?' A person who can *think* but is without the capacity for ordinary speech is still a difficult concept for people to accept. It seems necessary, therefore, to look into the nature of language in total before considering how thought processes work.

Behaviour is everywhere!

A chapter on *behaviour* follows. Strictly speaking, behaviour is anything we do, either voluntarily or involuntarily. Colloquially, however, it is more generally associated with *bad behaviour*. When we read headlines in the press about 'crowd behaviour' we are primed to expect the worst. It is another example of words which accrue to themselves adverse connotations – just as the practice has grown up recently of referring to 'weather' as meaning unpleasantness, as in 'Is there any weather about?'. As weather is a universal and constant system, of course there is weather *about* – literally! So there is behaviour about, especially when we do not remark upon it. Whatever the circumstances, however, 'standards of behaviour' is a phrase that leads us directly into the norms of a particular society. Certain behaviours are actions that social conventions proscribe as unacceptable or prescribe for acceptability and this raises the matter of the child with severe difficulties in the society in which education is taking place.

Normality

The pupils under focus in this book are not in any way viewed as *deviant*. They should rather be seen as experiencing an underexposed normality – as defined (or simply commonly accepted) by people in general. The focus is the normality. The *principles* refer to essential normality. The *detective work* referred to above is based on the premise that the first thing one looks for, in such an approach, is all the evidence there is of normal functioning and straightforward development. That is the first important thing to notice and record about a child; that which otherwise no one bothers to see simply because it is 'normal'.

Note, at this point, that it is not the age of a child that determines the normality of any action but its place in the general development sequence of our common humanity. The role of the educator is to try, by every means possible, to show the picture of the individual pupil with clarity as it emerges and with as much 'normality' as can be detected and then developed.

Finally, in slightly different form and as a summary of the ideas in the book, there is a discussion about how all these principles would underpin a meaningful *curriculum* as it is planned for pupils in severe difficulties with their learning.

Individualism

The pupils who are the focus for this book are all individuals. They are, indeed, pupils who can be observed to have difficulty in coming to terms with education as it is generally presented in schools (even in special schools) and with whom, in turn, teachers and classroom assistants find difficulty. They are, however, all individuals with idiosyncratic styles of learning and needs peculiar to themselves. Experience of many such children will, of course, give professionals an insight into common traits between various individuals; this is, after all, the basis of this book. Nevertheless, it is the comparison between individuals that determines this, not any categorisation according any one characteristic or label. The severity of the difficulty for staff working with the pupils may be taken to be more that of a difficulty of understanding how each individual's mind is working in its social context rather than any arbitrary point of difficulty along a scale from a normal child in a classroom to a child with what are termed profound and multiple needs. For convenience only, pupils who present with these difficulties to the imagination of adults will be referred to occasionally as 'pupils with severe difficulties in learning' in the hope that such difficulties will be lessened by the discussions which follow and ways will be found to enable them to realise the full potential of their capabilities.

Like all children, they may at times strike adults around as funny, depressed, exuberant, naughty, charming, irritating and the rest. I hope this book may contribute to their being enabled to pass out of the problem zone into the world of 'When you understand them, they're not *so* difficult after all'. More than that, however, is the hope that the pupils will be enabled, thereby, to be accepted as partners in reaching a potential that requires the skilled and insightful guidance of a thoughtful profession to unlock.

Notes

1   The *Oxford English Dictionary* defines *'principle'* (among other referents) as 'a fundamental quality which constitutes the source of action'; and it is in this sense that I am using the term in this book. Considering the basis from which thought and action should proceed has been the province of philosophy through the ages and many philosophers have set down their fundamental positions on both the purpose

and the practice of education. What constitutes those principles has fuelled ongoing debate, in Western culture, at least since the time of Plato. Setting out guidance for pedagogues in addressing the needs of their pupils became a prime focus of philosophical and religious thought in Europe in the fifteenth and sixteenth centuries, with its most illustrious champion the Moravian cleric Jan Amos Komenský (known more generally in English texts by his Latin name, Comenius). In his book *The Great Didactic* he set out a series of principles to underpin his recommendations of teaching methodology – some derived from the scientific thought of his day, some characteristic of his own personal philosophy. They formed a key element in what is known now as the humanist tradition of the time that led directly to the Enlightenment and the Age of Reason. My contention is that this recourse to thoughtful reason is the undercroft upon which educational practice should be built and where its wisdom should be stored. In this book are to be found the principles which I suggest form such a foundation for staff involved with pupils who are struggling towards learning. Some reflect a tradition that goes back directly to Komenský; for example, the idea that education should proceed from the whole to the part, not vice versa. Some come from experience over years in education; for example, the conviction that the basis for meeting any difficulty is to establish as far as is possible, the normality in the situation before deciding on programmes of exceptional intervention. They are not exhaustive and readers are invited to further study and contemplation in forming individual principles of their own upon which to establish, with confidence, their own educational action.

Further reading and study

For Jan Amos Komenský

His main educational work is generally translated into English, from the Latin Didactica Magna of 1657, as *The Great Didactic of John Amos Comenius*, a version of which was published in England in 1910 by A&C Black in translation by M. W. Keatinge; now available only in an edition from the USA, published by Kessinger Publishing Co. of Montana. A previous version of 1632 was written in Czech under the title *Didactica, to jest Umění umělého vyučování*.

For some of the current arguments from philosophy and sociology

Clark, C., Dyson, A. and Milward, A. (1998) *Theorising Special Education*. London: Routledge.

For contemporary and ongoing debate

The Journal of Philosophy of Education (Journal of the Philosophy of Education Society of Great Britain). Oxford: Blackwell Publishers.

CHAPTER 2

Principal Principles

> Their Principles are the same, though their modes of thinking are different! (Samuel Johnson)

What happens in everyday life to let it be a natural thing that infants present themselves for schooling of some kind as a perfectly acceptable event? I am not necessarily talking about formal education; there are many situations in the world where formal school either does not exist or is less accessible than the traditional upbringing of custom and usage in tribe or extended family. There is, however, in all social societies the powerful 'learning at mother's knee'. Sociologists and social reformers may point out what they consider to be the inadequacies of some early influences; but they cannot deny that the early influences are educative, in the broadest sense. It would be foolish, therefore, to believe that children came to school as empty vessels, having learned nothing and simply waiting to have formal knowledge poured into them. Early influences and genetic predisposition combine to determine what any child brings into formal instruction and from that early age the process of education is *interactive* (Tizard 1985). This chapter suggests what the principles are that underpin this interaction: the factors that predispose the developing infant to pick up knowledge from everyday social contacts – sometimes unsuspected by those who imagine they are the main teaching influences!

It is important to understand these principles when considering what pupils with severe difficulties are drawing from conventional schooling because one of the handicapping conditions they face is often that they are subjected to formal educational approaches before they have *experienced* the conditions for benefiting from an ordinarily structured curriculum. They do not readily learn because the educators – and I do not necessarily mean teachers but all those determining their development – do not consider that the children may be struggling with such *principles*.

It should be noted that in using the description 'handicapping' in the previous paragraph I am not carelessly using the term as a deleterious description of the child. Articulate people in disability awareness circles point out (and it is firmly the position taken in this book) that a child is a child is a child. It is society that handicaps a person by attitude and false superiority. The description is used here to make the same point: that difficulties are preserved when they are not understood 'from the inside out'.[1] The potential of all children is eroded if they are not helped by society to prepare themselves for that education which society bestows upon them, beginning with principal principles.

What, then, are the prerequisites that seem to come so naturally to most children but which may need additional nurturing in some?

Principles underpinning natural education

1. A sense of identity – 'I'.

2. A sense of curiosity.

3. A sense of experiment.

4. A means of exchange of ideas.

These four principles hang together as essential parts of the early development of a child. Indeed so natural are these steps in development that they attract no special notice in most children. It is usually in infancy, however, that absence of all or parts of these elements can be noticed and, indeed, where early attention to awaken them is likely to be of most benefit to a child. It is also the time when parents, having noticed that 'something is wrong' often report that nothing is done by the professional to whom they turn on the grounds that the child may 'grow out of it' or 'is not ready for help yet' (Cooper and Henderson 1973). These principles, however, are basic and observable as coming from within the child from birth. Any disquiet about their absence has to be taken seriously and addressed. Without them, education in any sense, formal or informal, will be a non-starter. Pupils may, indeed, be limited in what their brain organisation will allow them to do; but if these principles are impeded, then the child will be unable spontaneously to make use of what is going on in the world around unless focused help is at hand. A classroom will prove of little benefit to the child if these functions are assumed to be in place for all pupils but are not operational in his or her case.

The term 'principal principles' which heads this chapter is to be taken to mean that in all the specific areas which follow – *language, thinking* and *behaviour* – these principles must be applied even when not directly specified. They underpin all that will be read concerning both theory and methodological approaches.

First principle[2]

A sense of identity – 'I'

Early communication and identity and its deficiency in some conditions of mental disturbance is evidenced by the feeling on the part of the parents that a bond between their child and them is missing (Cooper and Henderson 1973). As we shall see, under 'Language', the early interaction that comes naturally to the human baby is the basis for its attracting caring to itself and its acceptance into the social circumstances within which all learning takes place. Lack of social signals, the lack indeed of establishing an individual identity, leaves the child as an outsider and, in social societies, outsiders do not flourish. The effects of lack of individuation (separation and asserting a personal identity) leads to an hiatus in the development process that, unless it is addressed somewhere along the line, will preclude social learning (Mahler 1969). In other words, without an 'I' (a sense of identity) the child does not learn *interactionally*. Under this restriction learning, at best, remains derivative and merely imitative. The consequence is that any instruction or exhortation to the child to be responsible for herself or himself is literally impossible to carry out. There is no sense of *self* for which a child can feel a responsible identity.

The matter of self-identity has, of course, been a subject for the attention of psychoanalysts. In the sense I mean it to be understood here, however, the realisation of self-identity is not to be thought of as separated out into the ego, the id and the libido according to any formulation of function (see for example Freud 1966) but to be taken more directly as a realisation that 'I am the person to whom the "I" pronoun refers. I control bits and pieces that I can see "out there" which are attached to me as arms and legs.' And, more abstractedly, 'I have things going on inside me that are not going on, necessarily, inside other people – ranging from simple emotions to complex pains in my stomach.' Nor is it 'egocentric' in the sense that Piaget uses the word in his investigations of a child's language and thought (Piaget 1959; Piaget and Inhelder 1969). The flavour of what I mean here is best thought of in connection with recent studies into what is known as the *theory of mind* (Wellman 1990; Whiten 1991); as being the necessary ability to realise that I have a mind and that there is something that is 'myself' in it. I have to come to the realisation that, before I can begin to interact with 'you' as another person in your own right, I too have to have my own identity. I shall consider the place of the *theory of mind* in more detail in Chapter 5.

Evidence of this sense is present remarkably early in most infants' lives; possibly it comes into the world with them and is not acquired so much as exercised. Studies of infant–mother interaction certainly suggest powerfully that this is so.[3] Sometimes, however, some disturbance in the mind impairs this realisation of self-identity and the infant's ability to indulge in interaction. This closes the door on its being exercised. In which case, a prime function of educational development is to excite it again. Unless (as a *principle*) it is excited, the educator leaves the pupil in a state of unresolvable bewilderment, surrounded by apparently random actions. Do not be deceived by acts of such a child that are described as 'self-willed'. Often they have nothing to do with any sense of 'myself against the world' but are reactions of extreme bewilderment.

Implication for teaching

Nothing could be harder than *instruction* in the use of the pronoun 'I'.

Consider this: 'Every time I use "I", I am not meaning the "you" that I wish to instruct in the use of "I" but the I who am telling you to use "I" about yourself speaking to me.' That is an illustration of how complex it is! Trying to *tell* a pupil how to use the 'I' form is equally complex.

The process of attempting direct instruction in the complicated use of the first person singular is likely to be mechanistic rather than linguistic and to be futile; because that is not how children develop the sense of who they are that allows them to *realise* that they each have an identity. If the object of education for pupils with severe difficulties is judiciously to replicate and reinforce the stages of development that might have been impaired or for some reason missed altogether, then it is necessary to follow the *detective work* outlined in Chapter 3 and pick up where the development seems to have come adrift. There will be no really beneficial education if it does not flow from the particular stage the child is at.

Growing identity awareness

In the pre-speech stage, early perceptions of separate and personal identity come from the infant's realisation that he or she has the power to alter the reactions of the humans around. Interactions, with adults from the outside world to early vocalisation that alters the body language around, raise a reaction of awareness in the infant that an observant adult might interpret as 'Hey! What d'you know! I did that!'. The growing awareness needs nurturing. In general development that is no problem. Babies cause reactions in the average adult that confirm to the child that he or she is of prime interest and some importance. This may not have happened, however, if the baby is too obviously different; not necessarily in facial features but in the body language that stimulates that reaction. Before a teacher or therapist can address any aspect of *identity* it is important to ensure, and if necessary to nurture, an awareness of the 'Hey! I did that!'. For pupils with severely dampened development, that may mean extending into the classroom how an adult would spontaneously interact with a baby in the crib. But here a note of caution is in order. I am not saying that one treats pupils of, say, the age of seven as babies. There are few things less respectful to the pupils in difficulties than being treated as if they remain always babies. What is under focus here is the *function*, not the form. To take one example: while it may not be appropriate to play a peek-a-boo game in class, the same message of 'now you see me now you don't' can be conveyed by making a game of eye glancing with amused facial expressions and a turn of the head. The function remains the same; the circumstances are appropriate.

The first location for a *linguistic identity* is 'I' within the mind and is developed through *inner speech*. Chapter 4 will consider in more detail the role of inner speech in the learning process; but for now, sufficient to realise that inner speech is the name for the language processing that goes on all the time in our minds and helps us to make sense of what is happening around us. Even as you read this chapter and consider your agreement or disagreement with its ideas, your mind is working with inner language. This mental habit is a useful means to give to staff a location into which to introduce the syntax of identity without the complexities instanced above.

Commentary and inner speech

The technique for enhancing inner speech is one of voicing what is happening as a commentary from *alongside* the pupil rather than in the more usual instructional position face to face. The teacher, as commentator, is then in the role of articulating what is happening, from simple activities such as looking at a book to complex matters of feelings and motives, in a way that is sharing with the pupil the practical use of the first person. Instructional language – 'Do this', 'Go there' – simply does not contain the possibility of identity. Indeed, it is worth remembering that the basis of military drill and parade-ground commands is deliberately designed to suppress the sense of identity and turn the individual into what is termed a fighting machine. Something different must be the basis for helping a child to the late development of a sense of self.

The only *instruction* that should enter into the process is the phrase: 'Say to yourself...'

Say to yourself: 'Look, I can see a rabbit in the photograph...there it is in the field...it's very small but I can just make it out...what else can I see?... This is a difficult picture to make out... I think it is blurry... I don't find it very interesting...'

Any contrived example such as this, of course, outside a real context, will seem forced and even patronising but the technique allows the most natural use of 'I' because the adult is both modelling it and, by revealing her own inner speech patterns, enabling the listening child to hear the correct use in a real situation. The gentle prodding of inner identity can be reinforced at any time in this way. Working alongside the pupil is important, not only because the speech is intimate, in the sense of being fed in as close to the ear as possible and without the distractions of visual signals via the pupil's eyes, but also because it lets the pupil into companionable workings of the teacher's mind. Up until such a point the pupil may not have realised that the teacher had a mind with which to interact!

Acts of identity

The first signs of identity, as we have seen, are discernible in the very early interactions with *mother* (and other caregivers). The problem for many children with severe difficulties is that this interactional dialogue does not take place. Nor do the dramas that act out identity development. Identity is nurtured, for example (as an extension of peek-a-boo), by an act of causing some distress in mother and really running away and hiding. Fortunately there is another powerful instinct that sets a limit to the length of an escapade before distress and loneliness set in and crying in mild panic betrays the hiding place; but the act has said 'Hey, I am someone apart from you'. The immobile child cannot do this. The child in difficulties is often not given the scope to do this. Of course I am not suggesting that the child is put in danger; but exploring space, running away within a fenced playground, for example, and gradually feeling alone and coming back, as all children will given patience on the part of the adult, is a necessary lesson in identity. The child who breaks out of confinement and runs far away – and therefore into danger – is often the child who has not been given an opportunity for controlled awareness at an appropriate time.

These factors of development happen before the syntactical use of the first person pronoun 'I' is firmly established and while the child may use a first name or nickname interchangeably, for a time, with the usage of 'Baby want... I like...', etc. These stages appear to be necessary for establishing a true sense of identity and practising its referents. Yet pupils with difficulties are often plunged into being made to practise the syntactical usage of 'I' before the *foundations* of selfhood have been sufficiently practised.

Teaching should start by ensuring that such practising can be absorbed and, as far as possible, built upon.

Eye contact

In this connection it is to be remembered that it is the *pupil* who needs to instigate the interaction if a sense of self is to be realised. If, to use again the peek-a-boo example, the teacher hides her face and then reappears it does nothing to alert the pupil to a sense of any other 'self' than that of the teacher. It is the pupil who has to be able to play a part in operating the game for it to be educative.

At this point it is appropriate to mention the matter of eye contact. It is a mistake always to insist that there must be direct eye contact with a pupil in every circumstance of a classroom. Eye contact should be an *act of will* on the part of the pupil and fostered as such. The game of hide-and-seek played with the eyes is a form of both willing contact and willing withdrawal of both parties and we all learn our social eye contact habits from the growth of such an original eye *dialogue*. It is this that establishes both the social benefits of 'paying attention' and the assertion of 'enough, let me be by myself for a second'. There is no point in telling pupils to ' Pay attention' unless the act of doing so, of *willingly attending*, excites an interest of the sort that, translated into inner speech says, 'Hey, there's something here that interests *me*'. What that thing may be depends on the developmental maturity of each pupil. It may not be enough for the teacher merely to be saying 'Hey, there's something here that interests *me*, children!' – especially if her body language and tone of voice belie it. The focusing of attention is important, as will become clearer in Chapter 5, but it has to be attracted; it cannot be commanded. The mere turning of the head and eyes towards the teacher is no guarantee that anything is being taken in by the pupil – whether the origin of such an action follows the instruction from a teacher or appears spontaneous on the part of the pupil; neither is it the case that *not* turning the head and eyes always means that information is being missed.

The pupil's use of 'I'

Merely using the syntactical form of the first person singular is no guarantee, by itself, that the pupil has a sense of identity in working order. This is especially true of children who have, perforce, had everything physical done for them since birth. Often all their potential decisions are made for them, with the best of intentions; clothes are selected and put on them, food is prepared and fed to them, 'interesting' displays are put before them to attract their attention and they are sat in front of the TV 'because they like it'. We must be very careful in saying what they like and dislike unless we are sure that these likes and dislikes come from their own *self*. Expressing a sense of self in words often requires some such sentence as 'I am certainly not going to wear that coat – I don't like it – oh, mummy, do I have to?' even if the result is, in the end, a lesson in social conformity and wearing the coat. Some children are taught to imitate sentences such as 'I like orange juice'; but that is no guarantee that they do like it. Spitting orange juice at the teacher may be the indication of *selfhood*: as it may be at mother with infants in a pre-speech stage.

Taking over

Having had the use of 'I' modelled as commentary by an adult, it then becomes significant as a test of the developmental process whether the pupil can take over the commentary. Maybe the pupil will use inner speech out loud – talking through an activity – but no matter. The essential point of development is that such speech demonstrates that the pupil is self-directing. Once a point is reached where there is a *self-correction*, indicated by a pause and some phrase such as 'No, silly, that doesn't go there!', then there is the beginning of evidence that the pupil is in tune with the second and third principles.

Second and third principles

A sense of curiosity and testing out the boundaries (experiment)

It follows that a sense of 'I' leads to the question of 'How do the world and 'I' relate?'. At first imperfectly identified, the question becomes more certain as it becomes established and gives a *reason* for interactional communication and a means of making *cumulative sense* of the growing world of impressions and experiences.

It proves impossible, in discussion, to separate the two aspects of being curious and seeing what will happen. And yet, there is a theoretical difference that we recognise between the two; the one internal and speculative the other translated into action. That seems to demand that they remain as separate principles. *Curiosity* can be, and in the sense of this chapter should be taken to be, an exercise of the mind. It is an intellectual action to speculate about what our senses take into our brains. In this respect, also, curiosity embraces positive wonderment at some new and pleasant sensation and tension and fear at an unpleasant one. It is the beginning of the reasoning process (Erikson 1978).

In all normal developmental processes, curiosity inevitably leads to *experiment*. There is *action* necessary, in the sense used here, in order for there to be experiment taking place. The role of 'play' in early development (Sheridan 1977) is an example of active involvement (*experiment*) flowing from the *mental exercise* of 'What would happen if...' (*curiosity*). It is more constructional than it is recreational, which is why it is a mistake to suggest that it is the opposite of 'work' in a classroom (Bruner 1976). Testing the 'I' against hypotheses about the world around is a skill that most infants cultivate from a very early age.

If they do not cultivate it, then their involvement in the world around is, literally, purposeless. The teacher cannot interrupt such bewildered purposelessness with instruction and expect the mind of a pupil simply to click into place. The normal development pattern is for years of purposeful curiosity and experiment to precede formal instruction; in the sense of schooling. There is, therefore a reawakening process necessary for a child for whom the pattern has been disrupted or failed to ignite. Care for these first three principles, taken together, must form the core of any methodology for helping pupils overcome severe developmental difficulties.

Implications for teaching

Developing curiosity into experiment

WHAT'S THAT?

Curiosity is only apparently passive because much of it is an activity *within the pupil*. This often makes it difficult to detect. When it comes to the surface is when a child is heard to ask, 'What's that?'. It is natural for developing children to have curiosity and any parent under ordinary circumstances will know the phase in early language development of the repetitious 'What's that?', and a little later 'Why's that?'; but for some pupils whose whole development has been inhibited in some way and whose language is outside regular developmental patterns, this phase may either not have been *experienced* (see Chapter 1) or more likely has atrophied because the means of communicating the curiosity has been absent and adults around have not actively sought for evidence of its existence. Many a child with profound difficulties is handicapped by adults assuming that nothing positive is going on in the mind until those adults impose a programme of their own devising. This is unlikely to be true.

The real difficulty for the pupil is often that the impulse to find out is present but, as it were, the brain does not know precisely what to do with it. Close observation of pupils with severe difficulties will often reveal a look of bewilderment fleetingly crossing their faces as they use their senses to mouth, finger, smell or otherwise seek sensory input from an object or a person. The look seems to say 'OK. It's here but what does it do or what do I do with it?'.

Now, that question is fundamental. If the pupil (any pupil) brings that question to a teacher, however communicated, then there is the beginning of dialogue which will be sustained as a basis no matter how ultimately sophisticated the matter of the relationship becomes. It is the same question that unites the profoundly impaired child and the PhD student within the process called 'education'.

The implication of this principle of curiosity, therefore, is that the role of the teacher is to excite it where it seems inadequate and nurture it whenever it is apparent. Because curiosity is largely an inner process, the challenge for the teacher is to reach the *inner child*. The process of doing this is an extension of the manner of encouraging the 'I': providing the commentary for the pupil.

Commentary extended

For many pupils it is important that the commentary, while working with the 'what?' and 'why?' also builds in reference to 'how?'. By this I mean that many severe learning difficulties stem from the inability of the brain to bring into direct comparison varied aspects of sensory perception in a useful and meaningful way. This will further be discussed in Chapter 5; but, for the moment, let it be taken as accepted that curiosity must expand to make links between experiences: or learning will not take place. It is often a role that the teacher must fulfil for pupils in difficulties: to make clear *how* to use information that undeveloped curiosity might have brought to the sensory notice of a pupil.

So it is not enough for a commentary to go 'Say to yourself, "I can feel this with my hand, this is *soft*"'. It must also go: 'Say to yourself, "I remember this is like the wool I felt yesterday; both this cushion and the wool in the jumper let me push my fingers into them. That's what I can call *soft*."'

In other words, to both excite latent curiosity and to satisfy it at the same time, the commentary introduces a model into the pupil's inner speech with a double objective: not only to convey information but to show what links with what.

In a similar way, it may be necessary to direct a pupil's focus upon that aspect of an event, artefact or picture which will yield the most information into the memory. Not all pupils with difficulties have sorted out which sense conveys what information. Guidance may be needed on what the teacher means by 'Listen' or 'Look' as well as clear messages about what the ears must listen *for* and probably specific information and finger pointing on to what the eye should focus *upon*. It is a remarkable feat of perception in the average child that allows for a series of coloured blotches on a piece of paper to be interpreted, without undue strain, as a dog in a basket. For some pupils, however, it may be more helpful not simply to say 'Say to yourself, "Look, I can see a dog in the picture"' but to say, 'Say to yourself, "I am looking at my finger tracing around the yellow bit with the brown spot – there – and I remember I called that shape yesterday a dog'".

From comment to experiment

Such a pedestrian approach, however, would, and therefore does, soon bore any children once they have got the hang of this curiosity thing. They are led by curiosity itself into *experimentation*. The essence of an experiment is asking the speculative question (in inner speech), 'I wonder what would happen if…' Therefore it is largely dependent on how far language has developed (see Chapter 4).

This development can be encouraged by staff modelling simultaneously both the actions and the language of playing around with material in an experimental way: 'Ask yourself, "What would happen if I put the red film over the green film and looked at the light?". Oh look. Now I can see…'

Apart from the fact that this is the essence of scientific experiment, it is also modelling actions, questions to ask and the discovery of possibly new vocabulary. The object of this exercise is, however, not so much to reach a valid scientific conclusion as to make experimentation mentally exciting when it has not functioned positively before.

Much of the experimentation of ordinarily developing children takes place in *play* situations. Play, therefore, is the practice ground for later and more formal classroom curricular learning. It must be realised, however, that what makes play such a profitable vehicle for the average child is that there is an in-built progression from curiosity to experimentation. The intention to play already exists, hard wired into the developmental system. Pupils with severe or profound difficulties, where language is delayed, may not be able to play *with a purpose* unless they have been helped with the inner speech of curiosity. If they have severe physical impairment they may not even be expected actively to play experimentally at all. Unless the teacher is herself setting up opportunities for curiosity that leads to fun, then a pupil may be spending profitless hours simply sitting and having things done to him or to her.

Pupils may be amused by the activities of the staff and may do as they are bidden – clapping on cue for example – but it is not play. All the play equipment in the sand tray will not even spark a glimmer of preparation for scientific learning unless a member of staff guides the pupils to find a purpose in an action. Pouring sand from one container to another or gazing at a wheel turning as sand is poured is not, of itself, evidence of 'play'. What is going on may merely be repetitive occupation unless there is a sense of enjoyment; which may be defined as the mental state of involvement in curiosity and experiment.

With a purpose

It is not the actions in the sand tray, however, that need to be altered but the sense of the actions having a purpose that has to be unfolded for the pupils. The role of the adult is to engender this sense of purpose and point to its application while still being a play partner and enjoying the situation. No matter what the age of the pupil, if there has not yet emerged a manifest ability to experiment, however simply, then any curricular work will remain moribund. That is how vital it is to kick-start the will to experiment as a fundamental principle of education.

Fourth principle

A means of exchange of ideas

There really is no point in isolated curiosity nor in experiments, the results of which cannot be shared. This is not to deny the role of *contemplation* in all our lives: the ability to work out our own curiosity in our own minds. Ultimately, however, there is an imperative to *share* the results. Young children can be observed to give adults the benefit of these thought processes, whether the adults are eager to receive them or not. Indeed, part of the social learning process for a three-year-old is to accumulate a sense of when the burgeoning thoughts can be shared and when it is a matter of 'Shush, dear!'.

Pupils in difficulties with conventional means of communication – speech in particular – are unable to convey readily to others what it is they are curious about, even when they are exercising curiosity; or what was the experimental purpose behind many of the things that they might do. They seldom hear a voice say, in response to an action, 'Well hello there! That was a smart piece of curiosity'. They are more likely to hear a disapproving 'Don't do that!'. Of course, there are times when it may be necessary to combine the two – 'That was a smart piece of curiosity but don't do it again, please!'. All the same the acknowledgement of a curiosity is important for development.

'Self' realised in a social context[4]

Clearly a child's behaviour in a social context depends on a realisation of *personal identity* and the *otherness* of the rest of the group. A sense of how to 'behave yourself' is dependent on a realisation both of the norms of the social grouping and of the fact that conforming is a conscious act under one's own control. This theme will be found again in Chapter 6 but the process of realising individual and social responsibility is a long one: the tension between *selfishness* and *responsibility* is not complete at least until maturity in adulthood. Much of the disquiet that we feel (if we are honest with ourselves) in the presence of children with 'difficulties' lies in our own difficulty in adjusting to signals which communicate their idiosyncratic sense of *self*. If, in reaction to this disquiet, we merely impose control from our selfish position, we are denying the very development of self in them. There will be a sense of 'self' to be found in all children if adults are sensitive to it and explore it with the pupil. The responsibility for finding the means of communicating the paths to social identity rests with teachers. In this sense, adults who work with pupils who are in severe difficulties with conventional ideas of learning must not lose their own sense of play and its purpose.

If the groundwork, of fostering identity and exciting curiosity, has been inadequately laid out, then the result is stultified performance rather than excited potential. Care must be taken lest the communication engendered and encouraged springs more from control on the part of the adult than it does from the fostering of self-expression in the pupil. Exchanges centre round what to eat, when to toilet, being quiet, rather than developing into the sort of diverse language play and interplay that a child with more usual development naturally uses. The characteristic of this latter is its variety both of form and content. As we shall see in Chapter 4, it is based, largely, on questioning and speculation as a basis for dialogue and thinking in stories (Wells 1986). It also contains, spontaneously, a vibrant sense of *fun*.

Fun and delight in communication[5]

It is worth considering how much fun is possible with the vocabulary that is supposed to be needful to ensure communication for pupils with no ready speech when they enter schooling. How is the pupil without ready speech helped to express complex feelings or make up a snatch of poetry? Denying to pupils in serious difficulties the possibility that they might want to compose poetry lacks respect. A good rule-of-thumb test for the effectiveness to the pupil of any communication system used in a classroom is whether it can, on occasions, be used to convey poetry and make jokes.

Implications for teaching

Communication

CONVEYING THE MESSAGE

Let us be clear from the outset that *communication* and *language* are not to be used as synonymous terms. The distinction between the two and the importance of language in development will be discussed in Chapter 4; and the crucial role of *inner speech* (that is, language functioning as thought, contemplation and curiosity) has already played a part in this discussion.

Fostering communication, however, is a principal principle of education because without it there can be no transmission between staff and pupils. Communication is the end product of systems within language that ensure that *meaning A* from the one party arrives as *meaning A* in the other(s). While a mix-up in the system which leaves the recipient acting on a mistaken reception of the message is often the source of rather cheap joking (the so-called 'howlers' in children's writing would be an example of this) it should be regarded rather as a serious breach of this principle if adults allow it to occur in a classroom. Especially with pupils who already have assessed difficulties, the importance of ensuring that the output message intended by the teacher is the same as the received message by the pupil is of vital importance if the pupils' difficulties are not to be compounded.

The most commonly considered transmission system for communication is, of course, speech (or its graphic equivalent, the written word). The vocalisation of speech, however, is but part of the whole communication process – even in an apparently simple dialogue. Because it is the system that most immediately comes to mind, people often forget that speech carries with it other elements which also bear upon what is communicated: tone of voice, facial tensions, the so-called 'body language', flesh tones, gesture and smell all contribute to the message and, for pupils for whom speech is not apparently the first ready means of transmitting communication, it is likely that these subordinate elements take on a prime significance. Thus, although the words of an adult may say, 'I like your picture very much' the other signals may convey dislike of the whole pupil; and it is the dislike not the praise that is the received message. There is no place to hide when a pupil is reliant on non-vocal transmission of messages.

Range of communication

For the full potential of a pupil to become apparent, however, he or she must have *experienced* as wide a range of received messages as possible and have been helped to communicate them back. Staff should beware if the staple diet of communication that pupils with difficulties receive is directive, even manipulative. The language, even as it poses as the communication of instructions for learning and classroom management, often slips into unrelieved direction and control. There is nothing wrong with judicious use of control, if for no other reason than that the safety of pupils demands it. The question, however, must also be asked: 'Do pupils experience the communication of emotions, lyricism, doubt, even of identity within such communication?'. It is for the introduction of the syntax of personal language as well as for inner thought processes that the technique of 'say to yourself' is so important.

This should also be a guiding star when a teacher is seeking to boost the communication within a group where speech is not readily apparent. I am not arguing here for one system of alternative communication against another – manual communication, communication boards, symbols and the like – but I am arguing for such systems to be used with a range of communicative intent and to be drawn up with the potential for communicating moods as well as wants. Not only do pupils need to know two-way communication about bananas and toilets, orange drinks and biscuits, work-time and play-time but they also need to have a means of exchanging communication about states (sadness, happiness, affection), desires ('I like Y', 'I can't stand X'), puzzlement ('Why? – there's no point I can see in doing it!'), and the inexplicable feeling of going out of one's own control. This latter is often communicated by a shattered door or a bitten hand when both the inner communication and the means of transmitting the inner confusion have not been fostered in the experiences given to pupils.

Moving on

The ability to communicate meaning, both in inner speech and in exchange of ideas, is essential to the process of education and self-control. It is fundamental to aspects of language itself, to thinking and to behaviour that are tackled in subsequent chapters.

Notes

1   The phrase 'inside out' which recurs throughout the approaches suggested in this book is used by the author, Donna Williams (1996), herself coming from within the autistic spectrum.

2   Because of the nature of autistic spectrum disorders there has been considerable attention devoted to the matter of identity and self-perception within the condition. Broadly the ideas put forward as this first principle reflect the debate in this field. By extension, the difficulties of some pupils with profound learning problems seem to me also to require study into self-identity.

3   The interaction of infant and mother (carer) was studied dramatically in the 1970s and this enabled much of the subsequent studies in infant social and linguistic development to go forward. They are crucial because they revealed the early competencies of infants and the role of interaction in normal cognitive and linguistic development which the principles in this book seek to reflect (see Schaffer 1977).

4   The social imperative as the basis for learning, which is fundamental to recent approaches to studies in cognition, recurs throughout this book, both as a possible impediment in those with learning difficulties and a mark of normal developmental stages which are fundamental to the principles put forward. Two recent books in which this theme is developed are Rogoff (1990) and Pollard (1996). Pollard also develops the sense of 'self' and the sense of 'socially other' that is merely touched upon in this book. For all children his theme of: 'How do young children become effective classroom learners? How do social factors, such as family life, friendships with other children and relationships with teachers, influence the fulfilment of children's learning potential?' (p.xi) applies no less to those with learning difficulties as to those in the mainstream of educational thought.

5   If fun needs any justification, then its place in linguistics and communication development is provided by David Crystal (1998). It is a sad reflection on the tensions that often accompany teaching schemes for pupils, thought to be in most difficulties with their learning, that fun seems to have absented itself from the educational process. There is an implied contrast between the grim task of learning (so much work to be completed) and a potential reward thereafter in the form of some fun. This is to put the cart before the horse. The principles in this book should be worked with fun as a key component – or they will not succeed. In the context of this section it can be stated that, if there is no means of communicating fun between staff and pupil, then the principle is not being applied.

Further reading and study

For 'inside out'
Williams, D. (1996) *Autism; An Inside-Out Approach.* London: Jessica Kingsley Publishers.

For the concept of self-identity
Jordan, R. and Powell, S. (1995) *Understanding and Teaching Children with Autism.* Chichester: Wiley.

For infant–mother social, linguistic and cognitive interaction
Schaffer, H. R. (ed) (1977) *Studies in Mother–Infant Interaction.* London: Academic Press.

For social contexts to learning
Rogoff, B. (1990) *Apprenticeship in Thinking.* New York: Oxford University Press.
Pollard, A. (with Filer, A.) (1996) *The Social World of Children's Learning.* London: Cassell.

For fun in communication and communicating fun
Crystal, D. (1998) *Language Play.* London: Penguin.

CHAPTER 3

Detective Stories

Between what matters and what seems to matter, how should the world we know judge wisely? (E. C. Bentley *Trent's Last Case*)

The role of anyone wishing to work 'from the inside out' and to gain an insight into the difficulties faced by a pupil with an apparently severe learning impairment is analogous to that of a detective in a detective story.

The detective, in a story, proceeds from *observation*, alert to the context of the enquiry and on the look-out for specific *clues* in order to be able to suggest ways forward in the dilemma of 'who done it?'.

The teacher seeking to identify the ways forward for a pupil with severe and complex difficulties in learning is also looking both for what is clear from the context and for clues that might only be seen by the observant and alert eye.

Because these ways forward, these slight differences, these idiosyncrasies in learning style, are specific to each individual pupil they will not necessarily conform to predetermined check-lists; although formal tests of one sort or another will doubtless have been over much of the ground. When there are puzzles and inconsistencies, it is sometimes necessary to break new ground, to reveal new aspects of a pupil's learning.

The difficulties into which the detective is called in fiction will not be routine – otherwise someone else would have solved them already. The circumstances are deliberately baffling but laden with clues for the person who is intent on teasing them out. The detective has always to appear confident but always to be alert to something having been missed.

The teacher, attempting to follow the *inside-out* pathway into understanding the complexities of the individual pupil's learning difficulties, is also involved in a process of working out solutions from clues that demand the keen eye of the observer and the experience gathered from other cases.

Of course the metaphor must not be pressed too far. On the one hand, no putative crime has been committed and on the other this is not merely fiction. It concerns the serious business of detecting the best way forward for each and every pupil. Nevertheless, the core idea holds good: that attention to detail, often missed except by the keen, aware eye, and looking for clues that are then interpreted with significance, is a necessary professional discipline for those who educate pupils with educational difficulties.

What follows in this chapter is not a schedule of classroom observation but a sort of starter kit for the classroom detective to alert the mind to where clues might lurk and to suggest what to make of them when they are detected. References back to the metaphor will be found occurring in subsequent chapters to point out where clues might be lurking unnoticed and how they might tie in with each other in forming the completed picture of where the pupil's difficulties lie.

Detective stories, of course, are not about real police crime solving. They are, by their nature, psychological 'games', pitting the reader against the writer in an intellectual maze. This is a good paradigm for work with pupils with severe difficulties. The adult observer is looking for *intellectual* clues in a way that a doctor or even a psychologist is not. Their role predominantly is diagnosis – police work, if you like. The teacher is more concerned with the little things that either facilitate or interrupt the pupil's ability to learn and, while the diagnosis is important (just like the story-detective uses the police files for fingerprints and forensic science), the real work for the teacher is in determining how the learning difficulty must be of this nature and only this nature (whatever is detected) for each child.

One of the best English writers in the genre of detective stories, G. K. Chesterton, set out in one of his stories a principle for the detective:

If you *know* what a man is doing, get in front of him; but if you want to guess what he's doing, keep behind him. Stray where he strays; stop when he stops; travel as slowly as he. Then you may see what he saw and may act as he acted. ('The Blue Cross'. *The Innocence of Father Brown*. London: Cassell (1911))

This can be adapted to fit the role of an observing educator. When a pupil is apparently learning and behaving more-or-less normally, then it is safe to present work in a more-or-less regular way. But when the pupil is showing that there are puzzling difficulties, then the observer must use *imagination*. Try to follow the lead of the child. Go, in imagination, where the child goes; make, in imagination, the same mistakes but maintain a critical intelligence while doing so. In such a pursuit the observing educator will find that there will be clues to the source of the difficulty – and, in the educational context, it may not be where a diagnostician might suspect. After all, it was the saying of no less a literary detective than Sherlock Holmes: 'that when you have eliminated the impossible, whatever remains, however improbable, must be the truth' (Arthur Conan Doyle, *A Study in Scarlet*).

The role of the detective/teacher's *intelligence* is, precisely, to eliminate the impossible, given the precise difficulties of the one particular child. The process of elimination of illogicalities is a constant theme in what I wish to put forward as principles in *language*, *thinking* and *behaviour*. The reader will find instances, in the development of the argument, where one factor (one clue) leads to one conclusion and eliminates others. Sometimes, however, such clarity is missed in lesson planning and target setting, with the result that both staff and pupil are bewildered by attempting to work with two incompatible notions. Looking for the logic that binds the clues, which are to be found by observing what is really happening, is the surer way to produce satisfactory programmes and raise individual pupil achievement. Attempting to find the *real* idiosyncrasies within the difficulties, *however initially improbable*, is the way to get at the truth.

Observation

To *observe* effectively the observer has to have a sharp sense of what to look out for and why.[1] As in most detective work, it is often the noticing of the small things that counts for the most. An important point of departure is that the observer goes into any observation without any preconceived notion of what to expect. Even when bombarded with a whole file of information from reports of others, the observer must blank the mind and focus strictly upon what is observable in the appropriate context. Time enough, when the details of the observation are established, to take the next step of working out how they fit into the reports and impressions of others. Please let it be noted, however, that I am not telling the observer arrogantly to ignore what others say. The discipline I am advocating is one of regulating the order of an effective detective procedure which ultimately works to the advantage of both the child and the adults involved: consider the pupil in as much detail as possible, imaginatively form an idea of what may be happening within the pupil, then compare this with what others have said and, finally, in the last stage of an observation, see if it all hangs together. If so, then well and good; the idea is a sound basis for planning a development programme. If not, then look particularly at the inconsistencies to detect how differing opinions may have arisen. Observe again, but this time focused upon the precise points that do not seem to hang together.

Clues

NOTES ON WHAT TO OBSERVE AND WHY

For the purposes of this argument I am not advocating any one method of structuring observation in preference to any other. I am aware of the constraints of both personnel and time in average classroom situations and that, however desirable it may be, releasing a member of staff to concentrate extended observations upon one pupil is fraught with difficulties. My advocacy of the metaphor of the detective is, rather, to encourage a state of mind; an awareness that is alert for the appearance of clues as matters proceed in day-to-day situations. By having an awareness of what to look for and therefore to have a recognition of what is unusual and of potential significance, the teacher is able to act both with more professional confidence and with more authority.

The principles set out in this book are based upon normal development and recognised patterns of difficulty. They form the context for observing pupils with awareness. What now follows in this chapter are patterns for more general awareness and hints on what to look out for and why. Overall impressions are important: the general appearance of the subject; build, physical characteristics and immediately obvious difficulties, if any. These, however, being generally obvious are likely to have been noted already in files. The telling observation, nevertheless, might be something slight and passing that the focused observer sees but which no one has bothered to record on file.

An example of this may well be the incidental evidence from body language which it is easy for staff to miss when their concentration is upon other pupils. It is often surprising how much information can be gathered from a pupil by the stolen surreptitious glance of an observer. Attitudes of bewilderment and disengagement or, on the contrary, curiosity and involvement are sometimes more obvious when the pupil is not under the direct attention of a member of staff. Particularly is it of interest to see how much indirect eye contact is being made and what the source of the interest may be.

Clues from the eyes are likely to be of significant use to the detective.

Eyes

Eyes tell us a lot. We pay attention to eyes more than to any other feature (Morris *et al.* 1979). At the same time they are often a source of preconceptions. Beware, therefore, of registering 'a wild look' or other vague phrases. What is to be observed are the characteristics of the eyes – their mobility or fixedness, their pupil size and variability, and so on.

Observe for:

1. Is the gaze fixed or mobile? What of the pupils of the eyes? What are the eyes *doing*?

2. How and when do the eyes make contact? Is it directly or sidelong?

3. Observable distinct eye behaviour linked to body language. Is the pupil looking around apparently unfocused?

The reasons for each observation are as follows.

FIXED OR MOBILE?

Gaze mobility may be a factor indicating that the pupils (in both meanings) are missing out on information. The function of the eyes is to feed to the brain information that, in turn, can be translated into meaning. From observation of what the pupil appears to be focused upon or even more tellingly not focused upon, and the subsequent actions, the detective can deduce whether the assumed intended message of the context is one that the pupil has grasped or whether another meaning has been registered. Mis-meaning is often an underlying cause of frustration for the staff and behavioural tensions for the pupil in class. Note: this is not a reference to eye defects. It is assumed that, if these are present, they will have been diagnosed already, although careful observation may suggest that certain so-far undiagnosed eye conditions may need to be referred on for further tests from skilled professionals.

The pupil (of the eye) varies according both to light and to the amount of information that the brain needs. Large pupils arrest attention by throwing a black cast into the eye. The glances eye-to-eye of lovers, when each is subconsciously trying to maximise the sight of the beloved, can be recognised by outsiders from this tendency. If, therefore, the eye of the subject strikes as particularly 'black', observe to see whether the pupils are responding naturally to light fluctuations – for example, when the child goes out into a sunlit playground or moves towards a window in class. If the pupils appear to stay large it should be recorded. It may indicate that the child is, as it were, over-trying to make sense of what is happening around but the brain is not processing the information it is receiving with sufficient competence. The result may be overload and the look of bewilderment on the face.

A caution is necessary about inattention. There are times when we all slip into a daze or daydream. We do so perhaps when we want to concentrate on an internal thought in our own mind and we shut out external influences. Context is most important in these cases. If, for example, the mind is not engaged by the information that is bombarding the eye or ear, a typically reported 'glazed look' (that is, apparent vacancy of the eye) creeps over the features. Often reported *inattention* in children in classes is a sign that they are totally unengaged by what is being set for them to do, in which case the difficulty is rather with the programme of work set than with the child. It is a fact that, without *engagement*, the child cannot learn and boredom will lead to complications. It is in the interest of both pupil and teacher alike that the observer records what the eyes are doing in the whole context of the lesson. There may be times when eye vacancy is a sign of epileptiform activity and, if *absence attacks* are suspected (O'Donohoe 1985), then again this is an indication that matters should be referred on. A characteristic observation in such episodes is that there are two distinct phases: the vacancy followed moments later by a sudden, noticeable act of attention (looking around, for instance) with an apparent puzzlement as if to indicate 'Hey! Where was I just then? What's going on?'.

THE WINDOW ON THE WORLD

The role of the eye is literally a window on the mind. Through the eyes we take in visual signals, masses of light waves, and rely on the brain to make sense of them. That is its job (Gregory 1990). But if there is a problem with the mechanism of making sense, then a child is likely to adopt various strategies (not necessarily consciously) to rectify the signal. Most clearly this can be seen when observing children with various types of already diagnosed visual impairment but they also occur in other circumstances; when the mechanisms of the eye are apparently normal and the confusion lies deeper into the brain mechanism. The clearest manifestation of such an adaptive, if involuntary, strategy is the so-called *gaze avoidance*. How this functions needs to be observed very carefully.

All people avoid one another's gaze at some time. If one observes infants very closely one sees eye contact verging on the extremes: from staring on the one hand to eye hiding on the other. Staring, 'fascinated' as we say, gives the nascent brain a large intake of information from which to extract data and match clues in order to make sense of what is going on. As a general rule, the more the novelty of the situation the greater the need for clues. Likewise, if the child suddenly becomes aware that circumstances have arisen in which something is expected but there is not sufficient store of visual images for comparison and therefore there can be no confidence in the match, the signal is averted by withdrawing the eyes – either behind mother's skirt, father's trouser leg or the cushion on the couch. Watch the child in these normal circumstances. He or she will typically keep peeping, taking in segments of the scene bit by bit, until gradually some general sense is made and perhaps a chance accommodation of images leads to exploration with more eye contact and indeed with closer physical investigation. It is all a question of maturity.

Also there may be a protectionist element in gaze avoidance: protection from mental pain. Mental pain has many origins. I am not meaning headaches from physical causes but the sort of tension which hurts and usually stems either from a rush of emotion, from what we call shyness or from what we call guilt and shame. Alternatively, as in some pupils with an autistic spectrum disorder, it may be because there are unpleasant sensations arising from the brain's inability to adjust to the signals that the eye takes in.

It is therefore important to attempt to distinguish, when observing, what might be the origin of any reported lack of eye contact. What is the quality of the contact that *is* made? It will be rare in the extreme that a sighted child makes no eye contact whatsoever with events. A useful tip for the observer is to employ the corner of one's own eye to note how often the subject steals a glance in one's direction when not directly being looked at and for how long such indirect eye contact is sustained.

REACTIONS TO WHAT THE EYE TAKES IN

The whole body is the field of reaction to what the eye sees. If the eye detects something that is a shock then the whole body characteristically reacts with various observable behaviours that, if analysed, indicate the level and substance of the shock. I may go rigid, I may burst out crying, I may scream – there are so many things I might do.

I have alluded already to this element of whole-body potential for communication that provides clues in which the detective can make imaginative deductions about the level of a pupil's ability to interact with what is going on around. In this respect, it is important to be alert to changes on the surrounding available signals. It is also important to attempt to determine how many of the signals are being understood by the pupil. Often it can be seen that a pupil is using eyes to keep up with a class activity even when there is ample aural signalling going on. Just because a pupil obeys instruction, it does not necessarily mean that he or she is acting on signals to the ear. A split-second delay, a glance at other pupils and then action may, in fact, indicate that it is the aural pathway that is a source of difficulty; in which case an entry in a pupil's record, 'Follows simple instructions', may be misleading and to the pupil's possible disadvantage.

Mouth

After the eyes the mouth is the next most frequent area of communication. Together with the eyes it transforms the face from a inert mass of flesh and bone into an instrument for conveying many and complex messages. We talk or make other noises come out, we 'pucker at the mouth', we yawn, we kiss – and so it goes on. We also smile and laugh. It is perhaps the smile and laugh that is most infectious, causing those around us to feel the urge to smile unless other more powerful emotions intervene. If these counter-emotions click in, we are inclined to scowl at the one who is all smiles. Over and above its role in *speech*, which will be considered in Chapter 4, it can act as a powerful mediator of communication. As with the eyes, however, the expectations of what a mouth will do can sometimes cause adults (and other children) to misread the signals that are centred around the mouth of a pupil with difficulties in learning.

Observe for:

1. 'mouthing' and what is taken to the mouth

2. any use of the mouth to make contact – kissing, biting, delicate lip contact that turns to a bite

3. the grin.

The reasons for each observation are as follows.

TASTE AND ONWARDS

We taste with the mouth – a most attractive and powerful impulse that alters from infancy into adulthood but never loses its basic urge. Because tasting loses its rank as one of the most important sense impulses (except for aesthetic and food responses) as we mature, it is easy for forget how powerful an instinct taste and smell is. Taste and smell can, for the purposes of observations, be taken as one and the same impulse. We have to attempt to discover, therefore, when a pupil is mouthing, whether it is an example of the progress of the principle of *exploration*. Clues may be garnered from what is taken into the mouth. Is it everything, or only, say, substances that can be moulded and manipulated?

In developmental terms, if everything is tasted or smelt then it is a clue that there is an educational need for other senses to be developed and evidence that these other senses have not yet been activated sufficiently for that pupil to be able to rely on the meanings that they generate in the brain. Caution needs to be exercised as to what is being taught to such pupils in lessons on taste. While it may be important to attempt to teach distinctions of taste (sweet/sour; nice/nasty, etc.) to pupils who are habitually mouthing, it is of more importance to develop other senses – sight, hearing and touch – as vehicles for information or there is a risk that the infant role of taste is overemphasised and growth does not take place.

MUSCULATURE

It is important to observe how tense the mouth muscles are when mouthing occurs. Especially is this true when self-biting is observed. Basically there are two possible configurations for hand biting – either of self or of another. The first is exemplified by rigid muscles locking on to the flesh and bone. The rigidity arises from a deep-brain instinct, locked into primitive hunting behaviour in flesh hunters (and the great apes all have this basic primitivism) where it is important to hang on. That causes locking on of the musculature. It is distressing to see and generally this instinct is directed outwardly into the flesh of others. If it has misfired, from some inner disruption, it will show in self-biting. Most mouthing, however, is likely to be observed as relaxed if persistent and mobile mouth movement. This can be accurately described as versions of licking, sucking and salivating, all signalled by this relaxed, if chewy, musculature.

The mouth, especially in developmental terms, also acts as a suppresser of pain or other emotions, as is the case when a baby bites on a teething ring or, indeed, where sometimes people stuff a hand in their mouth when pain is present somewhere in the body. The observer should be aware of mouth activity so that this possibility of its being a reaction to pain can be discussed when it comes to the attempt to work out what the clues mean.

MOUTH CONTACT

There are various mouthing habits that occur quite normally in many infants. *Thumb sucking* is a case in point. Objects are sometimes suckled in the way thumbs are; in a comfortable sort of way. There are children, in contrast, who apparently explore with the tongue and mouth, pushing into corners of awkward shapes and assiduously licking surfaces. Again there are children who take things right into the mouth. The observer should note (provided safety is not compromised) the nature of the object, texture, whether it is rolled around the mouth and so on. It will not be possible to work out what significance *mouthing* has to the pupil unless there is close observation of the subtleties that are grouped under this term.

Mouth contact has also to be observed and recorded factually. Let us take the common word kissing. Seldom can so many and various forms of human contact have been subsumed under one so all-embracing word. There is, as they say, kissing, and then there is *kissing*. Passionate kissing in lovers, greeting kissing in some cultures, 'giving grandma a kiss' in children. What is a pupil in difficulties to make of such diverse meanings to one action? Has the child sufficient inner reasoning to have the required level of awareness in what is going on? Is it more simply a basic bonding of infancy that may be persisting? The observer is not to be expected to jump to conclusions during the observation but it is important for subsequent discussion to expand the term 'kissing' into something more accurately and objectively descriptive of what is going on.

Similarly, the nature of other mouth-to-flesh contacts and their context must be objectively recorded. A *bite*, for instance, may follow upon a lick-and-smell session. What might be the cause? For subsequent discussion on possible interpretations of the behaviour it will be necessary to know, for example, whether the bite arose suddenly from a passing contact from apparently relaxed musculature (see above) or whether the bite contact was sudden, originating from a distance. Teeth contact to flesh, even in apparently relaxed mouthing, can trigger autonomic reactions deep in our hunter-gatherer past and for this reason it should be borne in mind that the most accurate description of a bite, sometimes, is as 'a kiss gone wrong'. Such evidence will give a background to discussion in Chapter 6 about what needs to be taught before biting can be 'corrected'.

THE GRIN

This is another area where the detective must be careful. The matter of 'the grin' is really another aspect of mouth musculature. What is sometimes reported as a pupil's grin is nothing of the sort. If the teeth are bared but the muscles taut, then it is a reaction of bewilderment bordering on fear. It is sometimes accompanied by the sound of what is called the nervous laugh. Such a laugh has no humour in it. Again, the clues as to whether a pupil is grinning and enjoying the joke or whether totally bewildered and fearful can be deduced from the tension observable in the musculature around the mouth. As a general rule of thumb, the tighter the muscles the more the fear and bewilderment. Observations can be cross-checked with the impressions left by whole-body language already discussed in this chapter. Unless other evidence can support the idea that the pupil understands complex interpersonal relationships that allow him or her to work out precisely how to effect anger in adults, then the apparent grin when the adult becomes disturbed is more likely to be fear of the change in the social tone of a lesson than it is a sign of self-satisfaction. This idea will be developed further in Chapter 5 under the discussion of the *theory of mind.*

Ears

It may seem that ears are not worth observing. After all, they do not move – except, occasionally, as the odd party trick! Nevertheless they form an entry, and an important one, for information to the brain. Children who have a history of recognised hearing impediment will have had a note made on their file. There remain, however, areas less clear. Is the child who is asking the teacher to repeat a question merely requiring more time to process information or suffering a problem in the passage of the voice to the brain and hence to the understanding? The main focus of observation for aural aspects of potential difficulty is, therefore, for evidence of the *effect* of possible impedance of the signals: for the understanding via the ears rather than upon the ear as an organ. What is the immediate action that the pupil takes in response to an aural input?

Observe for:

1. The child consistently turning to a neighbour to ask for a repetition of what the teacher said, or a look of bewilderment spreading into the eyes when the child is addressed directly.

2. The child sticking fingers in the ear as peripheral noise rises.

The reasons for each observation are as follows.

1. STATIC ON THE LINE

While this behaviour may indicate a deficit in the mechanism of hearing, at this stage in the observation it is not advisable to conclude what the deficit might be. The observer is not seeking to determine evidence of physiological or neural hearing loss as such (although if the evidence points to referring on, then that must be done) but rather a confusion in attention and in processing in the brain when aural signals are present. The observer is looking for clues that will indicate whether the pupil has been able to make sense 'in common' between adult and self. When a pupil is observed failing to carry out an instruction satisfactorily, the detective has to determine whether the evidence points to such a confusion in meaning. It is important to consider whether the confusion comes from the pupil's not having a grasp of what it means to *listen* rather than from any difficulties with the mechanism of the ear, as such.

The ability to listen effectively is a skill of *language* and *thinking* and will be a theme in Chapters 4 and 5. Sufficient here, when evidence gathering is the focus, to note that 'looking at teacher' is not the same as 'listening'. The clues as to whether a pupil has been listening can only be gathered from the evidence of that pupil's actions after the event.

2. HABITUATION

Such behaviour as this may indicate the reverse of too weak a sound signal to the brain. It may be that the brain is oversensitive to noise. There are children in whom the safety valve of *habituation* appears to be defective or absent (Tighe and Leaton 1976). Habituation is the cut-out that the brain uses so that it does not have to process all the signals coming in through the ear (or the eye and nose for that matter). It is what enables us to ignore the clock ticking in our dining-room when we are having dinner. The ticking will only impinge upon us when it stops! Too much noise would become quite unbearable and would need us to stick fingers (or cotton wool or almost anything) into ears to shut it out… Certain frequencies, too, are impossible easily to accommodate: in my case a tumble-dryer in the kitchen that puts me into an irritable mood because I cannot habituate to it. This is a matter of personal make-up, but there may be indication in children, especially those with profound difficulties and lack of ready communication skills, that sticking fingers in ears is a way of saying 'For goodness sake turn off that soothing music you think is good for me!'. The observer is looking to determine what is comfortable from the clues in the behaviour of a pupil, and the observation itself should be entered into as the adult's end of a communication exchange.

Co-ordination

This is a potentially complex area. It is not only the readily obvious that yields the potent clues to an observer, but also the more subtle and the partially hidden. By co-ordination here is meant *how the senses and the musculature combine*. A better term for the concept might have been 'integration' had this word not acquired a legitimate educational and administrative meaning of its own. A readily seen difficulty, for example, occurs in the pupil who cannot hit a ball, however broad the racquet – a mis-co-ordination of eye and brain signals to the forearm. Generally such clear instances are lumped together under the term 'clumsy'. The observer should beware of such a blanket term, adequate though it is for general staff room chat.

   Observe for:

1. handedness – consistency of use and of which hand

2. posture – apparently awkward sitting. Especially note any hunching and straining when looking down

3. confusions when attempting to carry out a movement (missing the target either when attempting to place things with the hand, kick with the foot or insert the body into a space)

4. 'Oddities'.

The reasons for each observation are as follows.

1. HEMISPHERIC DOMINANCE

Many perceptual confusions and disorganised processing in the brain can be traced to the degree of hemispheric dominance present (Bishop 1990). Knowing which hand is used and, indeed, if there is a preference is therefore important.[2] This information should be on file; but it is as well to check it out by observing for consistency of both the hand that is used and the foot that is used. Lack of a consistent use of a hand may be a sign that the pupil is genuinely ambidextrous but is unlikely if the pupil has drawn attention by being said to be clumsy.

2. CLUES FROM AWKWARDNESS

If the pupil has any degree of physical impairment it is to be hoped that a physiotherapist or an occupational therapist will have already advised on the correct sitting posture and the appropriate chair support. Some pupils without recognisable physical impairment, however, may still have observable posture difficulties. If a pupil has adopted apparently odd sitting positions, observe also for what the eyes are doing and how the hand and elbow are operating. Remember it is the combination of how the information is *transmitted* between the senses, the brain and motor movements that will gives clues for subsequent consideration.

Observe especially to determine whether awkward sitting may be a sign that the pupil has difficulty making sense of materials laid flat on the table in front. It is not generally realised just how difficult it is to adjust the focus of the eye to make sense of anything laid flat in front of us. This is especially true of the act of reading or making sense of text and pictures. When a teacher reads a book, naturally sitting at home, it is seldom if ever horizontally flat on a table and pushed up against her abdomen! Yet children are set tasks on this uncomfortable plane. Their reaction to this demand should be noted. Of course there are things that require flat working – writing, for example, is usually performed flat – but it is always worth an experiment to see if a pupil performs tasks the better when they are presented on an inclined plane.

3. WHY HESITATE?

It is important to be accurate in fixing a description of the context and sequence of a pupil's hesitation in a movement. Was it, for example, *frozen movement* – apparently going to carry out an action and losing it? Was it when the pupil was acting on a command or when the action was self-instigated, or both? If it was an action upon a command then the difficulty might be one of language processing but if the hesitation was in a movement that was started by the pupil, then the difficulty is likely to stem from underdeveloped body awareness. If the pupil seems to be in a state of wondering, 'Where are my hands and my feet?', then that may well be the difficulty he or she is facing. Self-orientation in space is so common as to be assumed in children after the age of approximately two years. In some children, however, the process becomes disorientated and this confusion manifests itself in apparent misjudgements with gaps, such as arm holes in clothes or spaces between tables.

4. IDIOSYNCRASIES

Oddities, by definition, are not easy to classify. I mean by 'oddities' those idiosyncratic movements – the slight dragging of a foot or the slight lean to one side, and so on – which characterise a particular pupil. These may only be individual traits, of no particular significance; or they might be of importance, for example as a sign of some neurological malfunction. Especially in matters of potential neurological dysfunction, it is important to have noted the often ignored *slight* tics, foot dragging, shakes, eye blinking and so on.

Behaviour

The problem of using a term such as behaviour is the multiplicity of references it carries with it. There is a tendency to use the term only in the context of something of which one disapproves. 'His behaviour is causing problems.' And while it may be true that certain aspects of the behaviour are annoying, even downright dangerous, the whole of what the pupil does is unlikely to be problematical. This matter is gone into in more depth in Chapter 6.

For the purposes of the detective, however, the observer, asked to concentrate on a pupil's behaviour, cannot afford simply to see what is irritating, annoying or otherwise adverse. Those may well be notable under a heading of 'the annoying bits of behaviour' but they will not be the sum total of the pupil's behaviour itself: that is, of all that the pupil does. There is a distinction to be drawn, for instance, between a *single item* of what a pupil does that, by itself, is so distasteful to all around that it colours, from then on, their whole view of the pupil, and a *series* of minor but irritating habits, the sum total of which is similar distaste. Often the clue as to why an item of behaviour is happening will emerge only from close observation of all the things that a pupil does over time. There is always a specific cause somewhere for conduct that is out of the ordinary but the cause may need to be traced to circumstances away from their immediate location. Until there are clues to the antecedence of an action, there cannot be confidence on remedial approaches.

It still remains true, however, that it is more important to know what a pupil with difficulties in learning can do than what a pupil cannot do. All too often concentration on observations of apparent defects leaves unremarked the positive behaviours (the skills and thought processes) that would give clues to the most appropriate personal way in to a pupil's learning.

The things that parents know

A vital link in building up the 'evidence' for antecedents of adverse behaviour and positive things to note comes from talking over, with those closely involved, the very early stages of a child's life. Much has happened in the days and months before a child may be seen by any practised educators. Much of the brain's development and consequent manifestations of cognition and language has happened before the child is two years old; and yet detailed educational observation may not commence until several years later. The gap can only be filled by careful, sensitive and focused dialogue with those who saw the child develop but may not have realised some of the significance of what was being witnessed. One approaches such memories with some caution. In the cases of early trauma, for instance, the memory for parents may be a saddening experience, reluctantly revisited. With care, however, it can and must be done because of the information that will perhaps provide the crucial clue to helping the child.[3]

Experience and the literature

Because each child with a severe learning difficulty or complex problem is a unique individual, combining difficulties with strengths and sharing some common developmental features with others, observers have to carry in their knapsacks, as it were, both access to the store of knowledge that already exists about the clues they uncover and their own hunches born of experience of other individuals they have known. To call them 'hunches' is perhaps to appear to undervalue what is a serious thought process; but at times it will not be possible to give chapter and verse for why one's thoughts are tending to follow a certain path. Sometimes it is a matter of seeing a resemblance in the actions of one pupil to those of a pupil observed many years previously. More often, it is the process of drawing on past observations, and sometimes past mistakes, combined with knowledge of the latest ideas and research information from sources within the literature.

Of course, no one person can experience everything. Part of the process of experience is being able to share and to benefit from the experiences of others who have been longer in the field or travelled in other field locations. In all good detective stories some character plays the part of the apprentice to the experienced eye of the detective himself or herself (to play Watson to a Holmes) and draws out the detective to reveal the significance of clues, to point out what experience saw that others, less experienced, had missed and to solve the mystery. The metaphor must not be pushed too far, of course. We are not dealing with an incident in time (a fictional crime) but with living and complex difficulties in a learning context. The idea that experience counts and others can learn from it, however, is a valid one. Each observer is both experienced and inexperienced and pupils benefit by the pooling of knowledge from a variety of sources. There is no room for blinkered thinking nor for adherence to one preconceived methodology or approach.

Ways forward

Having carefully gathered the clues and looked at them with the eye of experience, having, where necessary, looked into the literature on certain points of uncertainty or novelty, it is now time to suggest an outcome. Here, at the end, we differ somewhat from the typical detective story. There is no crime to solve but there needs to be an hypothesis about how the pupil's difficulties should be met. The way forward should be both obvious to the observer and convincingly explicable to others. The skilled detective will always try to nurse others to find the clues he or she has already seen and then to suggest, rather than dictate, a solution: 'Why don't we do...?'. If a programme is to succeed, it needs to be within the thought processes of all those who are to administer it. Nevertheless, it must always be remembered that all suggested solutions, even when supported by evidence, might have missed something and may not be the whole answer. A judicious mixture of confidence and caution is useful, as illustrated in perhaps the best of all the genre of detective stories in the English language – E.C. Bentley's *Trent's Last Case* – the opening sentence of which started this chapter.

Finally, it must not be forgotten that the focus is upon the individual pupil. It is not upon the difficulties but upon the difficulties as part of that individual pupil's natural make-up. And that pupil is not all difficulty and nothing else. Start always by being aware of what the pupil *can* do; by observing what is so usual as to be considered unremarkable. It is the one danger with descriptions of syndromes and their characteristics which diagnosticians use appropriately to name a pupil's difficulties that they may lead people to expect certain specific conduct in a pupil, even in the face of the evidence. 'He has autism therefore he must...' And so on. Concentrating on the principles of the *normal*, on keeping an awareness that what is generally not drawn to our attention may be of great importance, is the surest way to throw into relief what really is the core of a difficulty a pupil may be facing.

Remember the observation of Sherlock Holmes in the story from The Strand Magazine 1892–93:

'Is there any other point to which you would wish to draw my attention?'

'To the curious incident of the dog in the night time.'

'The dog did nothing in the night time.'

'That was the curious incident,' remarked Sherlock Holmes.

(Arthur Conan Doyle, *The Adventure of Silver Blaze*)

Notes

1   I have suggested that the notion of the 'normal development' of a child is the basis of what a teacher needs to work with. What follows in this chapter should always be referred back to the range of normal expectations in child development. As this is not a book specifically on child development the reader will need to look elsewhere for guidance. One of the clearest expositions of the *sequences* in growth and development that offer a clue to what to expect, what to aim for and what is apparently lacking is still *The Stycar Sequences* (Sheridan 1973). More particularly, and to focus on the contrasts between the typical and atypical developmental pathways, see Talay-Ongan (1998).

2   Hemispheric dominance in the brain – and its manifestation as handedness – is an important but technical subject. A good introduction is given in Bishop (1990).

3   To work with parents in an understanding and sensitive manner needs care. A useful guide, in the context of helping children with learning difficulties, is given by Burke and Cigno (1996). Staff need to be especially sensitive to the adjustments necessary when an event such as the birth of a child or a realisation by the family of 'something not quite right' in some way alters the expectations that preceded that event. This in no way suggests that the emotional joy of parenting is diminished. It is, however, an intellectual adjustment that, in more or less degree, all parents have to make to the realities presented by offspring with difficulties, and staff need to understand that such adjustments are being made all the time by parents of their pupils.

Further reading and study

For child development in a readable form with clear visual clues to help detection of what is normal and what should follow what

Sheridan, M. D. (1973) (and subsequent expanded editions) *From Birth to Five Years – Children's Developmental Progress*. London: Routledge.

Talay-Ongan, A. (1998) *Typical and Atypical Development in Early Childhood: The Fundamentals*. Leicester: The British Psychological Society.

For hemispheric influences in the brain

Bishop, D. V. M. (1990) *Handedness and Developmental Disorder*. Hove: Lawrence Erlbaum Associates.

For interaction with parents

Burke, P. and Cigno, K. (1996) *Support for Families: Helping Children with Learning Disabilities*. Aldershot: Avebury.

CHAPTER 4

Language

> The…basic assumption is that the most reasonable and practical hypothesis on which to base intervention goals is to be derived from what is known about normal language development. (M. Lahey 1988)

It is the underlying premise of this chapter that programmes to be used with pupils with severe learning difficulties must be constructed from linguistic principles and, to be effective, must reflect and reinforce the course of normal language development. Some attempts to marry linguistic insights and programmes for pupil development seem inadequate in that they do not go far enough back to basics to build up understanding in pupils with profound difficulties. While they may improve a pupil's apparent performance under controlled situations in a classroom, they do not necessarily reach the many processes that language is properly intended to supply. Goldbart (1986) makes a good attempt to show both the need for principles and the underlying need for linguistic analysis to underpin the construction of any programme. She goes on to note, however, that 'Unfortunately, the transfer of these ideas from academic theories of normal child language to classroom activities for teaching impaired or ineffective communicators has been slow' (p.153).

Too great a concentration on the outward performance of communication as a *behaviour* rather than the full implications of language as a *development* often seems to be the basis for interventions (Rosetti 1996) and is inadequate given the insights into linguistics now available.

Principles

The *principles* of language development that underlie the discussion which follows, then, will be these:

1. Language is instinctive – the capacity for language is hard wired. It has to be activated rather than learned.

   Corollary: Structures follow developmentally in a regular order (although the order itself may vary because it is specific to individual *languages = tongues*).

2. The development of the brain dictates when a pupil can use certain structures and form certain concepts.

3. Semantics (the refinement of meaning) goes from the larger to the smaller.

   Corollary 1: The idea of metaphor precedes exact definitions.

   Corollary 2: Thought comes before the capacity to *think with precision through language.*

4. Language has an inner function that differs from external communication in its intentions and working.

5. Inner language is generally in advance of the ability to utilise sophisticated expressive language.

6. Communication and language are not the same things but language is generally useful in communication.

   Corollary: Social interaction is also a necessary component for communication.

First principle

Language is instinctive

STRUCTURES FOLLOW EACH OTHER IN A REGULAR ORDER

There is a considerable body of study now that shows that language is an *instinct* (Pinker 1994; Pinker and Bloom 1992). The idea of language being learned from nothing – the 'empty vessel' idea – no longer has credence. It is clear that a child does not enter the world without language (Locke 1993) and simply wait for sounds to imitate and then graft meaning onto those sounds. The circuits for adult language are wired in (Hoekstra and Kooij 1988). All the drive for interaction (the underpinning of communication) is apparent from birth and has been understood with increasing clarity since the sophisticated research carried out in the middle of the last century and already alluded to in the Notes to Chapter 2 (Bullowa 1979; Schaffer 1977; Stern 1977).

In this sense, also, a child's first home language (or languages) cannot be *learned* (Toobey and Cosmides 1992). Circumstances allow a child to practise *language* in social interactions and by practising it and experimenting with it, to employ it with ever increasing sophistication. Each language (in the sense of 'tongue' – for example, English) develops according to a regular syntactical pattern. The stages a child habitually goes through in developing a sophisticated usage of the English language have been set out, for example, by Crystal, Fletcher and Garman (1976) and similar sequences exist for other languages (see, for example, Zimmer 1986). No one (in normal circumstances of family life, that is) sets out to give grammar lessons to a one-year-old; but there is evidence that one-year-old children already have the drive to impose order on the language around them and use it as a framework for the development of ideas (Bauer and Mandler 1992). Growth in brain capacity, in the rapid increase of synaptic connections, allows innate capacities to become more active and blossom into both social speech and inner thought. In that sense, there is no necessity for learning to follow teaching in the practice of using language. What learning there is must be seen as a naturalistic consequence of adapting to being a mature human being, a social interaction in parallel with all other social interactions in human development. It must be realised, therefore, that for pupils with severe difficulties in learning, the confusions in their social interactions and the confusions in their language are intertwined. It does not help them to so concentrate on instruction in language that the importance of the social context for its development is missed.

Implications for teaching

Language instinctively

ASSUME THE LANGUAGE CAPACITY IS INTACT

When confronted with apparent deficits in language, however severe they are, the teacher is best served if she assumes that the basis of language is more than likely already present and it is the *developmental mechanisms* that have misfired. The first teaching idea, therefore, is to assume that the *drive* to function with language is intact. The fault in the pupil's system is likely to be in the organisation of the component parts that bring language into recognisable form and use.

Having a 'hard-wired' drive to do something but not having the means is frustrating – deep-down frustrating. The first thing to do for any child who appears to lack outward linguistic expression, in the form of *speech*, is to tune in, with sensitivity, to all the tell-tale signs that the pupil manifests of what is basically *linguistic* activity. The importance of gathering such clues has been discussed in the previous chapter.

One of the most helpful developmental ways in which a teacher can consolidate the impulse towards language in frustrated pupils is to mirror the early *language interactions* of motherese (that is, the sort of interpersonal language used by carers to a child in the cot or on the knee before the child is fully verbal). This conveys to the infant a sense of being part of a linguistic society. It is therefore a paradigm for adaptation by staff seeking to activate language development where it has been impaired in their pupils (Crystal 1987).

The pattern of language, on the adult's part, is characterised by *ranges* in tones of voice and conversations in which the infant is included *as if a verbal participant*, and where the *topic* is varied – apparently randomly but, on closer examination, with an internal consistency that is relative to the context.

There is very little modelling occurring in the early stages. The infant is not told to 'Say X' because, of course, it is not expected that he or she will have the ability so to do at that stage. Instead the language is in the form of a sort of running commentary:

> OK – so you want to play – You think it's funny to blow bubbles, do you? Well I can blow bubbles back. And you think it's a game to pull my hair? Well I don't; and I think for that you can have

your tummy tickled. Oh no! There's no need to cry. I'm not angry so there's no need to feel upset. Come on, smile! What's the matter? Is there something really hurting? Or are you in a sad mood suddenly?

There are several points to note in such an exchange.

First, the adult is concerned (albeit without thinking) with the *emotional state* of the infant and addresses the child on the assumption that the emotional state is also recognised by him or by her. The tone of voice conveys this as much as the words do. It is mutuality, in that emotions are carried in the language used by the adult on behalf of both parties. There is no direct *instruction* because instruction carries a hostile, or at best emphatic, tone. It is all conversational, even though one-voiced and the willing participation of the infant is assumed.

Second, the language is explanatory and regulating, not proscriptive. The impulse of the instinct for language is to make sense of what is around into an ordered explanation of life. We shall consider how this order is itself usefully ordered when we look at the implications for teachers of the acts of *thinking*; but it is the efficiency of the grammar of language itself that allows order to be imposed. What is more, there has to be encouragement for it to be nurtured within the pupil as a natural consequence of growth. Early language directed towards infants has this element of *explanation* and *order* of the here and now. It is as if the adult is saying, in this one-voiced but two-participant conversation: 'Look here! This is how you make sense of everything from game-playing to astrophysics.'

This is the difference between developing language as a birthright ('home' languages in whatever profusion they may be naturally acquired in infancy) and learning a 'foreign' language at a later stage. In the latter we find the grammar, being taught rather than naturally developing, is frankly a chore because we are thinking about it rather than developing it spontaneously in a social context.

We have to beware lest the drive for 'speech' is imposed on pupils with severe communication difficulties as if their 'home' language was foreign. If pupils are given words as if in vocabulary lists and every 'mistake' is seized upon and corrected, then the socialising elements of explanation and order do not readily enter into the situation. This method of language 'training' reduces the pupil to a tourist in his or her own classroom. The impulse to correct often comes at the expense of the child's real need. The most notorious example of this in the literature is given by McNeill (1970). He quotes the following incident:

Child	Nobody don't like me
Mother	No, say 'nobody likes me'
	(eight repetitions of this dialogue)
Mother	No, now listen carefully;
	say 'nobody likes me'
Child	Oh! Nobody don't *likes* me

(p.107)

This is a desperately sad reflection of totally the wrong linguistic priorities. The child was not developmentally ready for the grammar but passionately needed mother to fling her arms around and say 'Nonsense dear, of course somebody likes you. I *love* you and that's better than like'.

The child would have absorbed the 'likes' form in mother's arms far more quickly than by a lesson on a too advanced stage of grammar.

At this point, and to avoid misunderstanding, let me say that I am not advocating that teachers fling their arms around pupils every time they perpetrate a syntactical inexactitude. The point is simply that language forms are instinctively linked to *context* in the learning process and sometimes it is the emotional meaning that is more important than the 'correct' use of the grammar.

I am not saying that a type of synthetic motherese should be used when the pupil concerned is 16 or even six, in exact imitation of the words and tone used with babies. I am saying that there has been, for most infants, a great deal of *language experience*, of which their linguistic instinct has enabled them to make use, before they ever come to a formal learning situation. In pupils with severe difficulties, however, this may not have been so and it is important for all staff to start working with them at a point where this instinct can activate useful experience (see the definition in Chapter 1). For some this will be, indeed, analogous to motherese, if information on the early development of a particular pupil suggests that there was no spontaneous interchanges in cot or pram or lap. For others, who have experienced early language dialogue, it may mean commencing the classroom interchanges at a developmental stage comparable with that of the language of an older infant. The point to remember, however, is that language development does not cut corners. Unless children are taken by the hand and led through natural sequences, what they will be left with will be an imperfect and probably inadequate language with which to make sense of their world. It is an arresting thought that many children who are considered of inferior intelligence, even granted brain damage, may be hampered more because their early instinct for language was not guided in a helpful and consecutive manner than by a poor result in an IQ test.

WORDS AND THINGS

Words that have an immediate social need develop first in an infant. Among the first (after identity games with mummy and daddy, siblings and a pet or two) are vital survival words such as 'more', 'algone', 'drink', 'no', and often some unexpected words that seem important for entering the priorities of the social scene because they crop up with frequency in family conversations. A child of my acquaintance used the word 'carburettor' as one of her first: her father was a garage mechanic and she sensed that the word had family currency. By contrast, the words commonly used in a classroom would not find their way into general conversation: 'sit here', 'get out your visual timetable', 'look at me', 'are we all ready?' (the tone of this last phrase, although the words form a question, indicates that it is in fact an instruction – 'be ready!').

Of course children have to be instructed in a school; but social aspects of language development need to be taken seriously before a pupil can set such instructional language in its proper context. This is so for no other reason than that language progress follows a set developmental sequence and it appears that children have to experience this sequence in all its steps in order to become established as truly linguistic. In planning the introduction of vocabulary, staff must be sensitive to a combination of the developmental stage of the child and the social context in which words and phrases are being used. It is particularly important when constructing *communication boards* for pupils without speech. A pupil, for example, may have a need to convey 'more' and 'go away, I don't like it' as being of greater use, both emotionally and pragmatically, than words the teacher might suppose.

ORGANISATION

Bear in mind that using syntax more complex than in the language of which the pupil in one way or another gives expressive evidence is doomed to increase the frustration of both pupil and teacher. As an example of what I mean, there really is no point in demanding of a pupil why he or she did something unless he or she has the developed ability to use a clause beginning with 'because'. All children develop through a stage where they realise that the word 'because' is expected as a response to a 'why?' question. But a considerable development in social and linguistic understanding has to have taken place before they realise that they are being asked to make explicit what was going on in their head at the time.

A grasp of what comes early on in language sequences (and what later) allows staff to monitor their own linguistic demands on pupils with difficulties and, because all teachers are focused on bringing pupils further along developmental pathways, gives them a set of benchmarks for evaluating progress. This is important when it comes to assessing progress in cognitive skills. It has been shown, by Donaldson (1986) that what a pupil can cope with is as much a matter of the language they are able to handle, developmentally, as it is of their thinking capacity. I have given an outline table of stages as a guide to progressive development in the Appendix. Monitoring the language used in classrooms, with sensitivity to pupils' development, is a better way of ensuring that they understand what they are being asked to do than is recording their failures to answer questions when they simply have not acquired the constructions to understand what the questions were all about.

Second principle

Look at the brain

Language accompanying growth of cognitive faculties will be dealt with in more detail in Chapter 5. What is important in the present discussion on language and the brain is that the innate capacity to become linguistic has to have the growth in fabric (as it were) with which to operate. If that fabric is impaired (and it may be impaired in any number of ways), then the language will not appear to have matured (Obler and Gjerlow 1999). It will have diverged from what is considered normal.

Let us look for a moment at the *brain*. The function of the brain is to make sense (that is, to take meaning from) incoming sensory signals. Some are mostly autonomic – controlling such impulses as variability in the aperture of the eye. Some, however, although still autonomic, are responses to social functioning like feelings of pleasure as reaction to the sight of a known comforter. There are, however, more conscious functions in which the brain is involved which are a combination of the physical capacity of the brain (as a organism) and a personalised outcome of its function, and this is generally referred to as *mind*.

In dealing with the concept of mind (Whiten 1991) we have to look both at the innate capacity for language which is present and at the social functioning that characterises human society. A child may be said, colloquially, to have a mind of its own but it does not make any sense to say that a child has a mind *on its own*. What would be its function and what developmental use would it have been in the progress of the species?

What we are looking at when we observe a child with apparently impaired language is not simply a child who has a limited vocabulary or does not make any sounds; we are looking at a manifestation of a complex but apparently confused brain system. Often what can be seen to be imperfectly functioning is the *self-concept* which allows the child to experience *self-awareness*, as we discussed in Chapter 2; in other words, to be able to express an awareness of herself or himself as a distinct entity and to use syntax in the first person. This generally arrives for a child at about two years of age, and while observations show that most children have an awareness of the *otherness* of a mother figure from birth, it is the self-realisation of that fact which takes time to become established in the language of the brain. Evidence of any apparent difficulty in the very early interactions between infant and mother figure is therefore vital in establishing how far the child may be in difficulties with a self-concept. (See 'The things that parents know' in Chapter 3). When we come on to consider communicative functions, we shall see that the drive towards communication arises also from social evolution and for it to make sense to us that we are distinct members of a shared culture, it follows that we must each have a firm concept of self. For most children this will be established in the developing brain as a consequence of growth, but sometimes it goes awry.

Implications for teaching
A matter of brain development
The instinct for language, although to be assumed in all pupils, has to be positively and sensitively fostered so that the pupils are given a developmental experience; and we have already defined experience as an act of being conscious of what is happening. If a pupil is left without the ability to put together thoughts that link and make cohesive sense, then some puzzling or absurd reactions are likely. Behaviours displayed by pupils with severe difficulties may be less to do with inherent deficits in the brain mechanism than with a lack of connected sequences of thoughts that make sense. The brain has to lay down patterns in *language* in order to make sense of the world in the way an adult does. The key idea here is 'laying down patterns'. It is for this reason that I am advocating studying and then seeking to reactivate that sequence of developmental steps that infants go through in order to equip themselves with a fully functional language, normally by the age of about four years of age. This is not a fully developed adult language but, for all practical purposes, the functions which are in place are capable of carrying the learning that the increasingly complex cognitive strategies, required in schools, demand. If pupils are not given a working access to these functions, however, then their thinking will not grow to best advantage and they will appear to be less capable than they potentially are. Education is all about pushing boundaries beyond the present level of a pupil into an expanding future. But it is unprofitable to put before a pupil work in which he or she is doomed to fail *because the brain is not yet organised to handle it.* The best guide to 'readiness' is to work from the · level of language organisation that a child exhibits along a developmental pathway, and to tailor a programme to draw the pupil, little by little, along the linguistic road.

To give one concrete example. The stages that an infant follows in establishing the grammar of a language – that is, laying down the pattern of language through which meaning will accumulate – is more or less the same for all children in any given 'tongue'. The 'one-word stage' and the 'two-word stage' are generally accepted colloquial ways of reference when an infant's progress is being discussed. Normally one stage blends seamlessly into the next until the child is conversing in more-or-less adult syntax by the age of about four years. Thereafter it is matter of refinement rather than acquisition. These stages are charted[1] and can be found in, for example, Crystal, Fletcher and Garman (1976). A summary of such a chart is given in the Appendix.

Let it be assumed that the pupil is using language (either in speech or signs) at a two-word stage. The chart outlines the various grammatical combinations that occur in child speech at this level and this, of itself, provides a paradigm for a teacher to check that a pupil is using all the various combinations ranging from a question form, 'What's that?', to a statement form, 'Dog go'; from a simple sentence, 'Daddy gone' to a simple description, 'Big car'. Note that we are not discussing *semantics* (meaning) here; that comes later in the chapter. We are looking for function and range. When a function is clearly present in the words a pupil uses then the teacher should extend the range of, say, the two words into a three-word function – 'That's right, the blue car (is) tooting'. By this stage, it is possible to draw out questions 'What is it doing?' because the form of a competent answer can be elicited from just a little way along the development pathway. And so on. It is the technique of 'accept from the pupil – extend: accept – extend'.

It is important to work to extend the organisational potential of language in order to facilitate the use of a pupil's mind. No matter how the brain may be technically damaged in the linguistic functioning, a pupil will still be striving to make sense (in the brain's interlinked language centres) of what is going on around. This is best done by striving to rehearse the categories of progress which a pupil may not have experienced and seeking to offer to the pupil increased organisation by employing the commentary approach outlined in Chapter 2. It is a safe enough rule of thumb that whatever grammatical function a pupil can use spontaneously can be extended one stage further by the surrounding adults along this developmental pathway.

Specific developmental 'blips'

There are, however, particular aspects of linguistic development in pupils with severe difficulties that seem to interfere with or to block what is the normal developmental pattern. These may require specific techniques from the teacher to either overcome them or to get round them.

IMMEDIATE ECHOLALIA

This describes the state in which the pupil appears to be stuck in reflecting back the last part of the immediate sound pattern heard, as in:

Adult   What is your name?

Child   ...your name?

While this is generally associated with autism it is also found among pupils with other difficulties. It is, however, a common stage in ordinary language development. What makes it into a potential difficulty, therefore, is not its presence but its persistence. It typically occurs as a phenomenon in ordinary language development, briefly, at the point where a child is on the cusp of confident *dialogue* but is inhibited by a combination of confusion in the reception of the syntax heard and a realisation of inner anxiety at being in society: the stage of *shyness*. Therefore, despite the fact that the pupil in difficulties may appear to show aggression rather than being a shrinking violet, the presence of immediate echolalia should always be taken to suggest the shy and be-wildered stage of normal linguistic and social development.

What the child in our example (above) is really saying is something along the lines of: 'Look here, is this a safe question? Is it an adult trap? Is my name really what this stranger is wanting? What does Mummy, whose hand I am holding, expect me to say?' (Mother prompts: 'Say Tommy!')

The child then, in saying 'Tommy', is, of course, indulging in immediate echolalia: but it is extended into social confidence in response to the child's confidence in the mother.

This stage is generally passed through quite quickly. Indeed, it is only in social situations that it is generally noticed because, right from the one-word stage, the child has been imitating and encouraged to imitate *the last thing heard.* Mother looking at a picture book and saying 'dog' expects immediate echolalia from the child. So, often, does the member of staff concentrating on vocabulary. If the echolalia gets stuck, however, and if it persists into school-aged children, the teacher is faced with the necessity of drawing the pupil through to the other side of this developmental stage.

As guidance on how and why to accelerate a pupil through, a teacher should bear in mind that what the young child is *meaning* by echoing in social situations is to signal confusion and ask for a prompt. Listening for a prompt, for guidance, is one of the assets that a teacher looks for in a pupil; it enables her to do her job of bringing the pupil on. Note that in the example of the child, the lady and mother (above) there are three actors and there always are in the 'confused' stage of echolalia as opposed to the expected echolalia in the one-to-one situation of looking at a picture book. While the teacher, therefore, can and does 'model' words in the one-to-one context, it is simply not possible, from within that context, effectively to draw a pupil through a delayed developmental stage of social immediate echolalia. It needs, initially, two people plus the pupil – the interlocutor and the prompter – to be compared to the questioning 'nice lady' and mother in the example above (Philips and Dyer 1977).

What the adults do is not really a technique so much as a strategy to ensure that the pupil realises the value and confidence building of echoing the right prompt. It works in this manner: Interlocutor (= teacher in this example): 'What am I pointing to?' Assistant (whispering into the ear of the pupil a split second before the sentence is ended): 'Tractor'. Pupil echoes 'Tractor' and is praised for it. Pleasure at right answer!

Contrast that small scene with what often happens in questions-expect-an-answer situations in class. The adult asks the pupil a question which the pupil half echoes. The adult is mildly annoyed and repeats (that is, echoes) the nub of the question 'Yes, yes, what's that?' If the pupil then echoes 'that' the locked-in echolalia has infected both parties and it simply cannot then be sorted out by the protagonists without much grief and confusion, making no linguistic progress at all. This is because the pupil is not being encouraged to go through a natural stage in language and social development – *listening for the prompt.*

I have no doubt that this strategy will meet criticism as being expensive in staff time: to use two adults for one pupil. The counter-argument is that the stage of *normal echolalia* in a child is very brief and so it is with pupils in difficulty. Once the brain is induced to paying attention to the prompt, indeed to listening out for it and echoing it in place of the question, echolalia *per se* fades and the next developmental language stage can be tapped into. The child begins to adjust the 'prompt' within the brain and another stage in the thinking process via language has been achieved. The key is that the prompt can gradually be given with less and less immediacy. The pupil will only seek for it when still internally unsure.

It has been assumed in the previous paragraphs that an adult is necessary to act as prompter. In increasing instances, the practice of sensitive *inclusive education* means that it can be a fellow pupil with more developed language who assists with the prompt. Socially this is a very powerful bonding strategy, broadening as it does the possibility for social-language dialogue. It is a benefit for both parties. The experienced pupil finds a role in guiding the less experienced and together they form a social context which, as we have seen, is a necessary ambience for the development of useful language.

DELAYED ECHOLALIA

This linguistic oddity is rather different from its immediate namesake. The term refers to the use by pupils of habitually repetitive language that seems to have its origins in a totally different social context. At first hearing it may appear to be random and have no immediate meaning. It can be exemplified by the pupil who suddenly shouts a phrase out of context. The speech is 'delayed' in the sense that it appears to be a throwback in the pupil's mind and it is echolalic in the sense that it is unmodified from someone else's original.

The safest approach is to assume that such speech derives from the instinct for social communication but has been garbled by a misfiring in the brain. In other words, it is not simple nonsense but may be useful. Functions that are not basically communicative may reflect an *externalised inner commentary*: that is, they may be an outpouring of what normally is an internalised thought process of the 'what is going on?'

variety. Various functional categories have been identified in the literature, including motor-habit functions that have no apparent communicable content (Dyer and Hadden 1981; Prizant 1983), but for practical purposes in the classroom with pupils with severe difficulties the teacher need only ask three basic questions and then act on the answers. Is the pupil:

1. attempting to communicate something relevant to the immediate context?

2. attempting to communicate a *change* of topic?

3. commenting to himself or herself – but out loud?

RELEVANCE

Relevance to the immediate context might reflect back to a link with an earlier incident which has stuck (functionally) in the brain. The important fact to remember is that such utterances have meaning for the utterer who has, in fact, generalised the semantics of a single situation in an attempt to make sense of varied social contexts. Kanner (1973), for example, cites the case of a girl whose mother used to attempt to stem her crying by pointing to a soft toy and saying 'Rabbits don't cry'. The girl later took over that expression and used the words, with substitute animals from time to time, as a sign that she was in a distressed state and likely to cry. Clearly, to help her, staff would have to know the referents and realise that 'Rabbits don't cry' was a call for comfort. To respond, 'That's right, dear, they don't cry', although factually correct, would be to ignore the girl's plea for emotional help. Such an ignoring might, in turn, increase tensions, convince the girl of her inability to convey what she intended and force her into communicative behaviour of a more violent and intense form. Liaison with parents and other carers to disentangle delayed echolalia is a special instance of detective work (Chapter 3).

Third principle

The quest for meaning

I wish, by this principle, to draw attention to the fact that semantics (the refinement of meaning) goes from the larger to the smaller. As a consequence of this, in normal language development the use of *metaphor* precedes exact definitions. It is in the quest to make sense of the world, also, that it is necessary for a *thought* to be present before the language that shapes it and makes sense of it.

Recent studies about the emergence of language and ideas about its origins have highlighted what should have been clear from the study of infant language development, which has occupied scholars and researchers since at least the seventeenth century. Infants do not construct language brick by brick, word by word, from a score of 0 to a vocabulary of many thousands, in less than three years on average, by learning a set number of single-reference sounds. Similarly, they do not work from single referent meanings, even as they use only single 'words'. The reverse, in fact. Even their single-word utterances carry a package of potential meaning. For instance, 'Dog' can mean 'That is a dog', 'I am excited because Fluff has come into the room', 'Help! I'm frightened'. Once more it is the social context of language that is important in establishing what exact meaning is present.

GO ANYWHERE

Once the 'three-word stage' of development is reached it heralds an explosion into sentences that can and do 'go anywhere'. Children begin the process of constructing their own story in the world they inhabit. They see their world as new and whole and then gradually refine it down to manageable single or conveniently related referents of meaning-to-words. The growth of language, as we have seen, is always within an orderly grammatical pattern; and by this order, within which to refine observations of the world and make sense of them, the child comes into a kingdom of power and potential that is a personal language.

Meaning is not built up from nothing: it is narrowed down from potentially everything (Cassirer 1946).[2] It has been observed throughout history, but strangely neglected by many educators, that to a child everything is possible and real. To children, that the moon is made of green cheese and that the moon is made of moon dust are equally possible. By about the age of six, at school, perhaps they will have sussed out that to teachers they have to give the answer, 'Moon dust, Miss' even as they listen, at other times in the school day, to stories about talking mice and actively sticky teddy bears.

THE CONCEPT OF STORY

Social life and social growth have always been couched in *story* and story is a realm of infinite possibility. In that sense, the child, as G. K. Chesterton (1936 p.52) said, 'understands the nature of art long before he understands the nature of argument'. To a child a story is not something that has to be extended from fact into fiction. It is fact, in fact, that has to be narrowed down from infinite possibility into specific and contextual definition. Adults do not lose that innate structure of *metaphor* – the capacity to make stories with which to think effectively; to see life as a winding road to the end of which we are enjoined to 'keep right on'; to see education as a stepladder and so on, even if these ideas are only at the back of our minds as we conduct apparently academic and soberly rational conversations. As Siegler (1996) points out: 'we organize much of our experience around metaphors. These metaphors are ordinarily unconscious, but they powerfully influence our thinking nonetheless' (p.237).

It is to be remembered, therefore, when we come to an attempt to help pupils in difficulties with language development, that it is not an insistence on vocabulary that will be most likely to help them but a means of helping them to develop the concept of 'story'.

Implications for teaching

The refinement of meaning goes from the larger to the smaller

The greater precedes the smaller, in the sense that children tend to be able to see the wood before seeing the fact that it is composed of trees. Again they tend to experience stories (in language) as being more real than the facts that fictionalise them. Reasoning, in its early stages, is more attuned to learning from random connections, as exemplified in fantasy, than from concrete certainties – fortunately for most adults who, in using language with children, happily have teddy bears speaking, dragons appearing over the horizon, firemen so wooden that propinquity to a real fire would char them irrevocably and railway tank engines representing their own youth rather than any actual sight the child might glimpse of one puffing through the countryside. Yet children absorb this language and gain from it; indeed, their sense of social intercourse is deliberately tutored by these stories even if their factual knowledge of railway practice in the twenty-first century is somewhat distorted.

SOCIAL CONTEXT

All this is a social preparation for thinking about *issues* rather than *facts*; and the majority of our daily linguistic usage, if we care to pause and think about it, is used for this purpose. Very little of the language of a day is occupied with discussing the precise wheel arrangement and gear ratio of the next bus. It is more usually concerned with speculation as to whether the bus will arrive or not. Stories are the linguistic plays of childhood which, together with physical play, prepare children for this world of issues. Therefore, I am arguing that there is a danger in narrowing down, to 'small factual steps', instruction in language development for pupils in difficulties with their learning.

To give room for experiment (see Chapter 2), on the other hand, is to tap into how a child's brain normally develops. When teachers start from the whole metaphor, as it were, the apparent difficulties take on new dimensions and pupils may then be able to demonstrate the capacity for thoughts which had long lain dormant. Thus I argue that children whose language is gaining ground only slowly do not need facts until they have had the chance to learn from story-play and fun. The skill of teaching is in so constructing 'stories' that the whole contains the parts that the teacher wishes to inculcate and the *language* that underpins this should be in the form (however apparently simple it has to be – see above) of a dialogue that leads the pupil from whole to part. As an example of what I mean, consider the steps used in teaching *number* to pupils who are having apparent difficulties in using language to make sense of social conventions. In the particular case of one-to-one correspondence it may seem useful for the record to test the pupil on ability to match cup with saucer, dog with kennel, red square with blue square and car with garage. But what is the story that can possibly give *meaning* to such a diverse collection of corresponding objects? Why should they correspond? Why should the dog not be in the garage and the cup in the car, carelessly dropped in the boot after a picnic? No reason at all; except that the answer is not based on the excitement of stories as a means of discovery but on a prejudged objective in a programme. Children learn, very early on, the real meaning of cup and saucer correspondence not by instruction, nor even practice, but by the nonsense of a mad hatter trying to drink from a cup on top of which an errant dormouse has stuck the saucer with impact glue and which, whenever you use it, must be handled with gloves on your paws! (Yes, I do know that that does not appear in *Alice* but we are playing with fiction about fiction!)

BUT WHY?

Again, it may seem obvious to a teacher that it is desirable to have, say, a 'red table' in the room. Everything thereon is red. But why? Wherever else in life do we gather things on the basis of their colour – except, of course, in the metaphor of a story? And yet the pupil who has just had to put cup to saucer because of the concept of tea-things (although his or her basis in experience might be of exclusively using mugs at home and cardboard beakers in McDonald's) now has to adjust to a classification not by form (which paired a red square and a blue square) but by colour, which pairs a square with a cup on redness alone! Without a metaphor to bind these abstract matters together in some cohesive form for cognitive processes, how can a pupil, already with learning difficulties, make sense of what is going on? Safer by far (it may seem to him or to her) simply to give up the confusing struggle. Therefore a pupil who is seemingly making little progress may simply have lost the metaphor and unless he or she is helped to find one again, then no amount of commanding to 'pay attention' will allow her or him to extract another iota of meaning from the lesson.

This is the sense in which the second corollary to this principle applies. Pupils have to have the metaphor with which to formulate potential referents *before* using inner language to reason out which might apply in questions before them. For this reason, as a basis for what is to be discussed in Chapter 6, the development of the *language* to codify the *meaning* that pupils make of life is one that needs to be understood and then fostered.

Knowing the answer first

Working from the larger to the smaller implies knowing an answer before ever a question is asked. The principle is seldom put in this way but in classroom activities, in any school and at any age, for pupils to create meaning out of lessons it must be so. The incessant questioning by young children of 'why this? why that?' means that they have answers (this and that before their eyes) but they have not yet constructed the language to come at a reason. Teachers generally ask questions, set problems and carry on general instruction in classes on the assumption that their pupils have the answer. Otherwise, what is the point of asking pupils to answer questions if it is known that they do not have the answer? With pupils in the greatest difficulties, however, it may be that they have missed out on the *developmental experiences* (see Chapter 1) that would have allowed them to gain the meanings upon which to draw in thinking about answers. The safest way of ensuring that they rectify this confusion is to give them the answers and then develop the metaphor and the language that can construct such answers (Meadows 1993): in other words, work from the sum of the parts to the individual parts themselves. It is analogous to working from a picture of the desired end product to the plans that allow it to be constructed.

To take an example: a series of sums can be set demanding that a pupil fills in the answers. This may be after several exercises building up to the number 4.

$$2 + 2 = ?; 3 + 1 = ?; 1 + 1 + 1 + 1 = ?; \text{ and so on}$$

The teacher knows the answer – that's why she is teacher! She has a concept of fourness, having been through experiences, probably even before attending school, which almost certainly involved counting games and playing with reactions to climbing stairs chanting, 'one, two, three, five'! Even on this simple level, when did most severely physically impaired children do that? By the time she reached college she had decided that anything set in the form x + y referred, in a solemn way, to such a concept of the specific reality of each sequential number in a maths lesson. But why should her pupils realise this, even if they can put '4' as an answer to each of the sums above? Without the experience of play and experiment and the language to go with it, it is probable that they will not realise it. The real answer to the sums above, therefore, *from the pupils' point of view,* is:

2 + 2 = I must say what teacher says and she says '4'

rather than any cognitive grasp, via language, that it is '4' because the metaphorical god of numbers assembled groups of people of various sizes and devised a game in which they had to stand on each other's shoulders and reach the treasure. I need not labour what is a not very imaginative beginning for a story but the point is made. The story is about the process and the social combinations necessary to reach the treasure '4'. It is climbing an intellectual staircase and there can be excitement and fun in making mistakes. And just think how exciting it will be making up the story for 1,000,000!

I emphasise, however, that this process has to be a dialogue; a *shared* language in the story. Processes in the mind do not come out of exercise books, nor off a computer. Consolidation of the meanings once glimpsed may well do so. In that sense, also, pupils must be helped to develop the skill to hold a dialogue within IT (Information Technology) and use the class computer screen as exploration. Most pupils now are fascinated by what can happen on a screen and have mechanical proficiency in gaining access to programmes; but for progress to be made they have to be guided into interactions with what they see and hear.

METAPHOR MEANS PROGRESS

The word 'story' itself is also by way of a metaphor. Visual experiences also work from the greater to the more precise; from the overarching to the particular rather than the other way round.

There is an account of this principle at work in a book (Pearson and Aloysius 1994) which describes the experiences of a class of teenagers, up to that point taught within the classrooms of a special school for the more apparently severely impaired learners, who were given the whole of the British Museum (under guidance – the Museum is a big place for anybody!) from which to make their own stories and within which to refine their own observations. As might have been expected (but I suspect was not) they understood what the experience was all about and were able to communicate, not always in speech but in drawing and other representational metaphors, important things like emotions, feelings and the sense of their individuality. The same class also had the experience of meeting the works of the artist Monet – not in the form of a single illustration in a book but on a visit to the garden at Giverny. From that there came their own delicate, individual and artistic appreciation of colour which, incidentally, some turned into much-sought-after silk screen cloths. The principle at work here can be taken as an example of providing sufficient *answers* (in this case, finished sculpture, the actual garden that inspired an artist and the contact with what he made of it). Upon these things their inner language could speculate and activate individual, personal responses.

Too often the presumed limitations of intelligence in pupils is the result of too limited a metaphor (a whole) within which the pupil can work.

Fourth principle

Language has an inner function

The preoccupation with the external manifestations of language – mainly speech, reading and writing – leads many people to assume that these are the *functions* of language. This is to ignore the fact that what we speak and what we write and how we read form only a minuscule part of the language we use in our waking and indeed in our sleeping hours. It follows from the principles above that much of language development takes place, as it were, in the head. Partly this is factor of brain maturity which will not finally resolve until puberty (Peel 1971) and partly a matter of the evolution of the conscious mind (Wellman 1990) which will be tackled more fully in Chapter 5.

We have already met the concept of *inner speech* in Chapter 2. The role of inner speech in the development of a child's linguistic competence was a main strand in the writing of the Russian psychologist (Vygotsky 1962; Daniels 1993). He puts linguistic emergence as a thought process somewhat late but, in essence, emphasises the importance of that language in which we each hold a dialogue with ourselves every time we work out notions as diverse as how much sugar to buy at the supermarket or the existence of God in the scientific universe. It is my contention, with this principle, that just as language is normally active from birth, so one of its basic areas of operation is this same inner speech. Both Piaget (1959) and Vygotsky (1962), writing before the seminal studies of early infant interaction (for example Schaffer 1977) were unaware of the insight into the active infant that such studies opened up. Their ideas, however, can be incorporated into the present argument. Both saw that language development was a synthesis of social experiences and the evolution therefrom of *inner meaning*.

To Vygotsky (1962), the process was evolutionary; the child refining the language around himself or herself, in the form of speech within social situations, into a personalised and competent usage in a parallel communicative and social development. He states, 'It is clear that ontogenetically thought and speech develop along separate lines and that at a certain point these lines meet' (p.50).

It is now clear, however, that the lines are more interwoven than might once have been thought. The child is active in a full spectrum of language within the mind and does not merely confine speech patterns to overt social use. Watch and listen to any child playing alone and you will hear words. Sometimes this will be an odd surfacing of an element from inner speech pattern and sometimes the full argument. Studies of young children's speech when on their own has opened a new door to understanding the nature of this inner process. In an elegant study of her two-and-a-half year old son's talking aloud to himself when left alone before he went to sleep Ruth Weir (1962) showed the component parts of this growing *self-dialogue* before it had become internalised. The externalised 'inner' dialogue peaked, as other researchers had predicted, at 2.7 years and thereafter internalisation soon followed. What is exciting about this closely observed two months, however, is the window it gives through which we can see inner speech functioning and glimpse its nature. The findings have since been confirmed in other studies (Nelson 1989).

One activity of this inner speech, little studied outside this research, is simply play: playing around with associations of sound and meaning, experimenting with collating various trains of thought triggered by various stimuli. Language is (or ought to be) basically fun to use. It clearly represented, for Weir's son, a rehearsal for using language to generate ideas. And it is in the realm of ideas that we shall again meet this inner dialogue in Chapter 5.

What is on view in Weir (1962) and Nelson (1989) is subtly more than the egocentric function described by both Piaget (1959) and Vygotsky (1962); which they saw as a preparation for adult social speech. It is the preparation for our *idiolect*[3] our own distinct functional language that we shall all use for the rest of our lives, although usually in the secret places of our mind. Think, however, of how we often 'talk ourselves through' difficult new enterprises, like finding our way in a strange town, and suddenly become conscious that we are talking out loud but to ourselves, and you will hear a minute instance of the inner speech externalising.

It is convenient, now, to take the next principle together with this one and then discuss teaching implications, together.

Fifth principle
Inner language is generally in advance of expressive language

It is true that children understand more of the language coming at them than they are able to give back in developed form but that, as will be shown in Chapter 5, is because they can think before ever they can turn thoughts into linguistically constructed communication. And it stands to reason that children have to be aware of at least one significance of a word before being able to use it as a part of their own communicative vocabulary. Here, however, we must make a distinction between the child's instinct for ordering social interactions in language and the growth of experiential knowledge that comes simply with the maturing process. That the child has a language capacity from before birth is without question; that the child has in place a complete dictionary is manifest nonsense. It is the language capacity that enables the child to enter into the process of sorting out meaning from the sounds around; linking what goes with what. The rhythms of those sounds determine semantic boundaries and refining down the referents made by the sounds (Menn and Stoel-Gammon 1995) is part of the developed progress that we discussed under the fourth principle. Very soon, of course, the child begins experimenting with the growing knowledge in a social context; throwing out a sound to see whether it functions in accordance with this inner understanding, and adding each refinement in line with growing understanding. (In this I follow Vygotsky.)

It necessarily follows from the idea that metaphor is present as the groundwork for this refinement of ideas-in-sound which are bombarding the child. It has been observed frequently, not least by Piaget (1959) and Vygotsky (1962), that children work from too large and idiosyncratic a span in their referents for sounds (*schemas*) and gradually become more contextually selective. A world in which all living things can be 'horse' or 'dog' or both simultaneously holds a great prospect for fun but, in the end, harsh reality dictates that one selected meaning per event has to be decided upon and stuck to if the child is to survive in a social world. It is, therefore, an appreciation of the meanings commonly present in the language around that enables children to find their place in a social world. This, in turn, emerges out of the wealth of potential understanding that they have begun to play around with.

Implications for teaching

The inner function of language

Putting words to thought is the inner function of language. It is often this *thought process* that is impaired in conditions of apparent learning disability, not the thinking itself. The process involves not only turning these thoughts into words but also turning them in such a way that they are communicable to others. Finding the words and finding the form of communication, therefore, are the two chief areas of potential impediment in everyday classroom performance of pupils with the most pressing difficulties.

Because, for all practical purposes, these two distinct aspects of language-in-the-mind are two sides of the same coin, it is possible to take them together in this discussion. Nevertheless it is important to remember that they are distinct and ability to function in one when there is an impediment in the other may be a cause of many *frustration behaviours* (see Chapter 6) that are met with in pupils with severe difficulties. The pupil whose thinking *capacity* is intact but whose capacity to *convey* thoughts is incapacitated is clearly in a most frustrating plight.

This state is sometimes found in those who have been victims of accidents where there has been injury to part of the brain to such an extent that speech is impaired but awareness is not. A careful piece of detective work can sometimes reveal that behind minimal and apparently ritualistic speech is a consciousness that is unable to bring thought into a cohesive and communicable form. When there is physical injury as well, with perhaps consequent epileptiform activity, then the pupil is indeed locked into a tragic situation.

INNER LANGUAGE

Generally the vehicle for thought-into-speech is *inner language* and it is a necessary and powerful vehicle both for processes inside the head and processes outside. When, therefore, it appears to be malfunctioning to some extent, it needs reinforcing.

There are three processes which staff can try to reach and reinforce:

1. inner *definition* as a means of understanding the world

2. inner language as a means of clarifying *intention*

3. inner language as a *companion and comfort.*

The first, developmentally, needs to be functioning adequately before a pupil can form thoughts into an expressive pattern; and, hence, it is normal for a pupil to seem to understand more than can be expressed. Putting it simply, but obviously, a pupil has to have been able to form a thought or intention and to have found the words for it *before* that thought or intention can be conveyed. Otherwise the pupil is left with one of two reactions as the only alternative to meaningful dialogue – a blank stare or the ritual words 'Don't know'.

It is a mistake, however, for staff so to concentrate on the expressive side of speech that its performance in a pupil distracts the adult from monitoring the functioning of inner language. Progress in expressive language (speech) is easier to monitor than other aspects of the whole linguistic package; therefore teachers may be trapped into believing that the number of words that a pupil produces (word counts) will give a reliable clue to progress. It may do so; but then again, it may not. Only if the pupil is using increasingly more words with clearly more intention and more understanding of depth of meaning will it be safe to utilise the shorthand of judging progress by word counts. This is a fertile area for detective work.

INNER DEFINITION AS A MEANS OF UNDERSTANDING THE WORLD

In seeking to enhance *inner definition* for pupils in difficulties the teacher should be seeking to accelerate the developmental progress that normally happens as words acquire meaning in the life of a child. Remember, however, that simply not being able to express language in spoken form need not mean that the pupil is unable to work with *inner language*. We have seen how meaning progresses from the larger to the smaller; from the particular word used for a whole class of objects or ideas to the classification and sub-classification that isolates 'cow' from other examples of the term 'animal' for which the child had originally used it, and so on. This narrowing down, in the normal course of development, is not generally directly taught; it is part of the process that happens in the early social contacts of childhood. Therefore, if the process has been disturbed, or has not started because of some brain mis-adjustment, then an attempt to kick-start it needs to be planned with the aim of bringing the pupil into the social, linguistic, developmental atmosphere which may not have been experienced.

The main nurturing grounds for language are the everyday conversations within which a child develops; not necessarily by being involved directly but by being within the surroundings. Therefore there needs to be a chance for 'conversational' language in the learning environment. In the normal course of events a child uses private soliloquies to experiment with the conversational language heard during the day and shapes it into some meaningful reference that can then be practised at some future time as expressive language. Conversation with a teddy bear or in bed with the lights out are noted in the literature as examples of this. The soliloquies use the language form that imitates the conversations heard in the course of the child's life, but essentially the child is practising inner language.

'Conversational' language is about *process* and pupils in difficulties need a teacher to let them in on the secret of how to process inner language. We have already glimpsed this process in a previous discussion on commentary (see Chapter 2).

Now let us see: if we take this and look at it carefully…look!…we can see a squiggly bit here (let's feel it; that's good!) and now if we look at the form board – we can try to see the squiggly bit in one of the holes – yes (look, I'll show you!)…and then we can try to fit the piece into the… *Yes*. Now let's have some fun and try to fit the piece in other holes…no won't go here…or here…or here! So now we can say to ourselves: we've found out that the clue to fitting it is in the *shape*.

Do not be put off by the written example of conversation. It does not read well until we realise that we seldom hear ourselves articulating our inner language and scarcely realise that we are holding a conversation with ourselves.

The beauty of conversational language is that it arises out of the social moment. Note, however, that what is implicit in the extract above is that the teacher is externalising her own inner language in the first person plural; taking the pupil's hand, linguistically, on a walk through a process. The walk and the pathway are infinitely variable to suit the subject. The teacher is pointing out, in the course of the model, precisely which area of focus will be profitable in order to reach a meaning in the particular context, what to look for, how to set it into verbal shape.

In language development, this is a way to exemplify for pupils the processes that, ordinarily, would link language and play and underpin curiosity and experiment (see Chapter 2). It also introduces the idea of how to have fun with the proof that there was only one way to solve the problem. Inner language is a great place for fun; for experimenting by juxtaposing bizarre combinations either of definitions or word sounds. It is the process that lies behind the string of apparently meaningless and even annoying sound patterns that, at a certain stage in development, children delight in. It is the process that makes deliberate mistakes as a joke; after all, you have to know the right answer to be able to mess it up deliberately. One of the functions of a teacher in cultivating latent inner language in pupils with severe difficulties should be to help them to play verbal jokes and to be silly. Of course, there is a time and a place for being silly. All of us have had to learn that, sometimes to our bewildered embarrassment in a social context, but it is, indeed, a learning process and needs to have been gone through.

Staff also need to use conversations with pupils as much about abstract definitions as they do about concrete form boards. (Indeed, concrete form boards would be heavy; too heavy for a pupil to carry! Our use of the word in this sense, however, gives some taste of the metaphorical route that makes *concrete* casually usable as the opposite of *abstract* and why children in difficulties need kindly explanation, in the first person, from teacher to work it all out.)

Unless pupils begin to be stirred by using language as the vehicle of thought they will not develop; but in order to use language in this way they have to be able to develop their own inner dialogue, and they will not understand how this inner dialogue works unless teachers exemplify the workings for them.

INNER LANGUAGE AND INTENTION

Incorporated into the conversation (above) was also a focus, in passing, on the *intention* of the process. Where do I mean it to go to?

Intention needs to be handled very carefully when teaching pupils with complex difficulties. Intention is a product in inner language; of my saying to myself, 'I have thought about this and now I am going to do X'. Without such a thought I am not in charge of myself, I am under a compulsion that makes me act from habit rather than my will. Examples of acting *unintentionally* in language abound, from the coprolalia in a few pupils with Tourette's syndrome (Leckman and Cohen 1994) to the slips of the tongue that often produce hilarious results in conversation. We have already seen how it is unwise to judge the actions of pupils when the syntax encapsulating the idea is beyond their developmental level. This now adds a further linguistic aspect to consider, which will need to be in our minds when we discuss behaviour (Chapter 6). To be responsible, pupils also need to have the capacity for forming an intention.

The formulating of an intention uses the syntactic construction 'because'. To answer the question 'Why did you do that? Why?' the pupil has to be able to structure his or her inner language within a 'because' clause. Becoming practised in this construction is not easy. For some time in their development all children grope for the usage, often appearing to assume that the word itself is sufficient reason: 'I did it because'. If, therefore, it is daunting for the average child to have to realise what is expected in answer to a question on intentionality, how much the more confusing is it made for pupils in difficulties?

Again it is to be noted that direct instruction can never teach a pupil how to personalise 'because'. An understanding of *self* (see First principal principle) has to be in place before a pupil can formulate personal reasons for actions and interactions. And until the pupil can formulate personal reasons in inner language, then there is no intention.

Usage from the language around is the key. How much conversation among adults in a classroom contains exchanges outlining reasons for what they are doing? For few pupils with limited vocabulary is the word 'because' introduced as part either of their (limited) sign system or their communication boards. Without the word itself and adequate words to follow it, they have no chance of incorporating it into their inner language and understanding. For any pupil in a school, however, the concept of 'because' is of immense daily consequence. More often than not, it is implied. Pupils are expected to comprehend why adults act as they do and why things appear to happen suddenly and randomly. It is little wonder that confused behaviour results.

As an example of the inner confusion, take a situation that we may sometimes find ourselves in; in which we do not comprehend 'because'. We are standing (in our imagination – our inner language) on a foreign railway station platform. Suddenly there is an announcement over the public address system. The passengers around us immediately show all the outward signs of consternation, pick up their luggage and rush towards the stairs. Why? We do not know. We do not understand more than a few words of the language and we cannot piece together in our minds the intention behind such a situation. We cannot say to ourselves, 'They are anxiously moving away from the platform *because...*'. We might follow but we would follow without any intentionality other than a vague hope that we would make some sense of what was going on along the way. Welcome to the world of many children in developmental language difficulties!

Conversational modelling of intentionality on the teacher's part is, therefore, both necessary for the pupils and a useful reminder to staff to make their intentions clear. Its by-product is designed to be twofold: by sharing experiences in the first person ('We are doing it because...') the pupils are prepared both to develop the inner syntax of intention and also to realise that actions have antecedents and consequences. This dual realisation is essential for cognitive thought. Moreover, without the means of conveying 'because' the pupils can never demonstrate that they understand such connectivity. The lexicon must contain 'because' for use very early on in any introduced sign system or alternative communication system (such as communication boards) and relevant accompanying vocabulary.

INNER LANGUAGE AS A COMPANION AND COMFORT

One of the insights that can be gleaned from studies of pre-sleep soliloquies of children in normal language development (Weir 1962; Nelson 1989) is the role that they play in enabling a child to work out tensions and stabilise emotions. Indeed, the role of a cuddly toy often has this as a function. The teddy bear is a comfort not only because it is warm and cuddly but also because it readily listens to the child 'getting it off his chest'. When a child comes late to the development of speech there is a danger that this teddy-bear conversation has not been experienced and so the child is left without the practice of using inner language for comfort and companionship. It is not sentimental on a teacher's part to take a child in distress and to say, 'Come on; let's tell Teddy all about it' – provided, of course, that this is an age-appropriate social behaviour. If the pupil is possibly aware enough that he or she is past talking to a cuddly toy (in public, that is – we are never past it in private) then the language still has to be modelled and encouraged.

In this connection I was given a cautionary lesson by some pupils from a primary school in a 'rough' downtown district where I had been invited to talk to the children about epilepsy so that they might understand and help one of their number. As my assistant I had taken along a large family teddy bear: by name Euston. (Well, someone else had already used Paddington!) At the end I told them that I would answer any questions if any pupils would care to wait behind. Many did and by the look on the faces of the staff I deduced that these were largely the 'tough guys' of the school. But a promise is a promise and I turned my attention to them. They waited remarkably patiently and one at a time came forward. The question that the majority asked was, 'Please can I cuddle Euston?'

If there really is an inhibition about age and teddy bears, however, the situation might turn into, 'Come on let's tell' (a favoured adult or a peer-friend), with the teacher attempting to model the inner language (thoughts) of the pupil, especially if that pupil has little or no overt speech.

It is precisely here that we can see the importance of the fifth principle and why it is in the canon. It has to be assumed that the inner workings of the mind of a pupil in severe difficulties need inner language in order to make sense: that they are present but, as it were, trapped. A skilled teacher will often talk to the mind of a pupil in trying to reach this inner process. Of course, such 'talk to the mind' is based on assumptions. The teacher has to use all the clues available (see Chapter 3) in an attempt to put into words what the pupil may be thinking and feeling, but it should be done. It should *not* be done, however, in the third person. The object of the conversation is that the teacher can identify with the pupil and therefore must use the language of identity.

There is a world of a difference between language which is framed like this:

You're feeling angry because you couldn't have your own way.

and

I know, I know. It's a rotten feeling being angry and not knowing why. Let's try to talk it out. When I feel like that I say to myself, 'That might be because I...'.

In the former the pupil is certainly being given a reason for a feeling but is not being given the personal language to cope with it. In the latter, the teacher is exposing the inner language process that she herself uses and, thereby, models also its syntax and form. The former, from the pupil's point of view, goes nowhere in developmental terms: the latter gives the pupil the framework for using language as comfort and for constructing a personal 'because' clause. It uses language to relieve the pressure of thoughts that are present but have no means of articulation and can be burdensome.

Sixth principle

Communication and language

SOCIAL INTERACTION AS A NECESSARY COMPONENT FOR COMMUNICATION

We have seen that language is an instinct. It might be truer, however, to say that *social interaction* is truly what is embedded into the brain. Language is the human evolutionary consequence of a social impulse that ensured the survival and development of the human race.[4] The ability to influence other members of the race and to 'read' their intentions is part of normal make-up (Lieberman 1998).

A simple glance at how we communicate with each other makes it clear that *ordered language* is but a part of the whole process. Even when we take language to involve more than vocabulary and extend study into *tone* and *rhythm* there remains what is referred to as 'body language' and, at a more primitive level, physical aspects of social intercourse of which we may not be aware. The main component of *communication* remains the use of language in speech sounds as the most efficient manner of conveying and discovering intentions in the social context. Quite a way down the line, in evolutionary terms, come graphic encoding of that language and only recently the ability to span distances of time and place with an immediacy undreamed of even a half-century ago.

Children who manifest difficulties with language are often, carelessly, termed 'non-communicating'. It is, in fact, rare for a child to be genuinely unable to communicate. Elements of the basic instinct for communication are almost always detectable if they are looked for. In special cases of difficulties, as for instance with some rare instances among children with autism, the instinct may be so subdued as to require very careful detective work; but so powerful is the impulse in animate beings for survival, that some communicative ability can usually be found.

Implications for teaching

Language and communication are not identical

This point need not be laboured. Sufficient should now have been written above to establish that the prime function of language is to form thought even before it can be communicated. Yet teachers are still taught that the purpose and definition of language refers to 'an organised set of symbols which in normal development is used primarily for communication' (Flack *et al.* 1996 p.3). While it is true that inner language must assume some recognised symbolic form (for example words) in order to become an interpersonal vehicle for social exchanges, and it is also true that the teacher has to be able to communicate to the pupil this symbolic form of inner language, as in the example we considered in the last section, nevertheless there is a danger in putting the emphasis so fixedly on communication. The danger lies in constructing classroom programmes of intended language development from the wrong end.

Adults must always beware of working with a programme which appears to be saying 'I will give you a list of words that you can use to communicate to me that which I want you to communicate to me'. The best of the programmes try to take account of the assumed needs of the child first but still, in the necessary course of classroom control, may let the balance shift into narrow and prescriptive channels.

The corollary to this principle states that a necessary component in communication is social interaction; in other words, linguistic give and take. It is this element that should first be nurtured in any concerted programme for language development, by whatever overt means. This priority acts as a safeguard against working with a limiting and prescriptive vocabulary.

There are many ways of arousing language in a socially communicative way, many of which have been touched on in this chapter. One proven way of relating mind and language to encourage both a realisation of and a practice of social dialogue is to help pupils to play with hand puppets. This is an opportunity for the pupils to externalise inner speech because the whole dialogue comes from their thoughts, but it also provides a context in which they can be guided into the realisation that social communication has to take account of what another person (the puppet) might be thinking. The character on the hand is visually distinct and yet the pupil has to enter into the mind of this distinct being in order to give it a voice. And it should be fun!

Another safeguard against a *control vocabulary* becoming the sole vehicle of communication in language development in a classroom is to ensure that, for every necessary control word or sign, there is a *gossip* word or sign introduced. The exact vocabulary will depend on the personality of the pupil, of course, but the general idea is that for every time the pupil is targeted to learn and use '(I want the) toilet' he or she is also targeted to learn and use '(I) like (your) hat'!

All that has been said before in this chapter is centred on the notion that what is happening in normal language development goes on mostly inside the mind of the developing child and in a social context of family, peers, experiences in general and, finally, in private reflection. For any child in apparent language difficulty – that is, who is not readily perceived by others as a communicator in language – the aim of the teaching process has to be to activate, or reactivate, the *instinctive organisation of meaning* through language which the mind provides. When the mind is activated, the pupil will have something worth communicating.

Notes

1   The sequence in which the grammar of English is normally acquired was tabulated in 1976 by Crystal, Fletcher and Garman. Originally worked on in connection with the rehabilitation of language in victims of strokes by rediscovery of the natural sequences of language development, it has proved a useful tool for those involved in encouraging language when it has apparently failed to develop spontaneously. The publication set out the Language Assessment, Remediation and Screening Procedure (LARSP) for obtaining language profiles as an aid to detecting aphasias and other specific disorders. This is useful, but cumbersome and time consuming for the ordinary run of classroom teaching. What I have attempted to do in the Appendix to this book is to map out some key markers to look out for and anticipate as a pupil develops through the stages that are normally followed. These, in turn, should form the framework for considering the way language is presented to a pupil in the classroom and act as markers for any specific bits that appear to be missing. In more general matters of language development in children I also suggest further reading for those who wish to go into the matter in more depth than is possible here.

2   Cassirer (1946) was a philosopher interested in the linguistic foundation of myth and spirituality. In doing so he opened up consideration of the understanding (the inner language) that makes universal meanings ultimately containable within fixed referents by the development of stories (myths) and therefore more prosaically by metaphors. This idea can be traced through many cultures and myriad 'tongues'. This approach now underpins the study of semantics: the quest for the understanding of how we understand meaning in language by refining down rather than building up.

3   The idea of *idiolect* is defined in the literature as 'the linguistic system as found in a single speaker' (Crystal 1987 p.24). I am suggesting here, however, that it is of more importance in working with pupils in difficulty than merely being thought of as that individuality of voice and style which means that we can be recognised by

acquaintances, for example over a telephone line. We all use language in subtly differing ways that make us recognisable in voice, in writing and in patterns of our conversation and argument. It is a common fact, but of little further import in the literature on linguistics, even if it assumes importance in literary criticism. Here I am suggesting that it ought to be of more importance when there is a language delay and lack of development in a pupil. For a true personality to develop the pupil must be led to use individualised language, not merely parrot-like speech and stereotyped phraseology. The realisation of 'I', which was discussed as a principal principle, demands that a pupil is encouraged to develop her or his own way of showing personality in language.

4   'Why language?' is now much under discussion along evolutionary lines, following the ideas of Charles Darwin. Basically, language *per se* must have had a survival imperative to have evolved universally as it has. The whole matter of physical and linguistic evolution from fossil to *Homo sapiens* has recently been explored by Lieberman (1998).

Further reading and study

For child language development

Crystal, D., Fletcher, P. and Garman, M. (1976) *The Grammatical Analysis of Language Disability.* London: Arnold.

Fletcher, P. and MacWhinney, B. (eds) (1995) *The Handbook of Child Language.* Oxford: Blackwell.

Foster-Cohen, S. H. (1999) *An Introduction to Child Language Development.* London: Longman.

For semantics

Wierzbicka, A. (1996) *Semantics: Primes and Universals.* Oxford: Oxford University Press.

For language and evolution

Lieberman, P. (1998) *Eve Spoke: Human Language and Human Evolution.* London: Picador.

CHAPTER 5

Thinking

Ah, but a man's reach should exceed his grasp,
Or what's a Heaven for?

(Andrea del Sarto, Robert Browning)

Education should not be concerned with the here and now, other than as a starting point. It is essentially all about potential – a leading onward (Latin *educare,* to draw out) and moving forward; about exciting and fostering the aptitude, from the phrase 'ability and aptitude' (Butler 1971) – rather than limited by any present apparent lack of ability. It is now generally accepted that the processes determining thought and language in children are hard wired in the brain (Toobey and Cosmides 1992) and that what is of the most interest, in both linguistic and psychological research, is the interactional circumstances by which both are refined and developed.

Active pupils

The child, independent of apparent IQ, is the *actor* in the process of learning and not a passive vessel into which educators pour carefully measured doses of knowledge for absorption and quantified outcome. Learning, therefore, is the end product of a vibrant exchange of thought through *dialogue* (as we saw in Chapter 4 – both with others and within oneself) and only in the sense of 'general knowledge' is it measurable as stored facts. The difference between not having learned something and having realised one has learned it is, in fact, a mere point in time: and that point is reached by and is the product of strategies that employ *observation, memory, speculation, experiment, confirmation* and *acceptance*; in other words, cognitive skills. Although the phrase is sometimes used, there is no true meaning to 'half-learning' something. Learning is simply not like that (Toobey and Cosmides 1992). The more unfortunate, therefore, that another phrase grew up in education circles (Tansley and Gulliford 1960; Williams 1970) labelling as *slow learners* those in difficulties with the process of schooling. Although some tried to gloss its use as meaning 'slow to *learn*' (Griffin 1978) most usage tended to concentrate on the 'slow' (Dyer 1991). The result was that much instruction for pupils with severe difficulties was slowed down on the assumption that they needed slow exercises with everything broken down into minute steps. It took time for it to be realised that the cognitive processes involved in coming to the point of learning could not function unless there was some dynamic action (in the brain), some fusing of ideas and some active interchange with other minds in the process. The more slowly the images are presented and the smaller the sectors under focus the less chance a pupil has of perceiving the whole circle.

I have argued in Chapter 4 that what governs the pathway into perception is the stage in language development and that perception itself flows from the greater to the smaller – from metaphor to dictionary definition, not the other way round. If that is so, then an adult is not helping a child to learn by preventing the vision of the whole road in concentrating only on small steps.[1] All children, whatever their IQ, employ a variety of approaches to tasks and ideas and make choices between them in building up working schemas for daily living. Recent research has confirmed that the fundamental strategic approach to a task is the same in all children (Geary and Brown 1991). The performance will differ and some pupils will require more guidance and help when they have difficulties in selecting which strategies the conventions of a task require. The help, however, does not come from making everything small and slow but from understanding how the thinking process in individual pupils is working and how to reach the points of confusion.

With that in mind we can look at the significance of some principles for the strategies termed 'thinking'.

Principles

1. Thinking is the mechanism through which all useful learning takes place.

2. Thinking is all about making conscious sense of incoming stimuli to the brain.

3. Thinking occurs in a social and cultural context and is defined by it.

4. Thinking and language operate as two sides of the same coin.

5. To be an effective thinker a person must be able to think about thinking.

   Corollary: Thought deals both with actuality and with possibility.

First principle

Thinking: the mechanism for all useful learning

SPECULATION

We have seen in Chapter 4 that children's language potential comes with them down the birth canal. So does their potential for thinking. The difficulties faced by children in apparently severe trouble with their learning, therefore, should be understood as inherent but possibly defective *mechanisms* that need adjustment in some way, rather than as blank and clueless voids that need filling in a painstaking and laborious fashion. There is a link between difficulties in language and difficulties in thinking that does have the appearance of one-to-one correspondence because much of human thinking is a product of the mechanism of *inner speech* which has been discussed on pp.79–83. As Donaldson (1992) states, the use of language excites the possibility of speculation (see Chapter 2, 'Principal principles') through which learning is fostered.

> Human thought deals with how things are, or at least how they seem to us to be, but it does this in ways that typically entail some sense of how they are not – or not yet. It deals with actuality and with possibility…achieved by the characteristically human means of asking questions. Is it like this? or perhaps like that? (p.9)

It is of importance that children who find difficulties in their learning are guided into positions where they are constrained to speculate. Again, as we saw in the Chapter 4, the child with difficulties has to have the *mechanism* for questioning nurtured and seen as of more fundamental usefulness than indicating apparent 'need'. As all parents (and others) will testify, the average child of three spends much of a conversation with an adult interminably wanting to hear 'Why...why...why?'. It is an imperative that fuels thinking. That which applies to the thinking processes of pupils in general applies equally to those who find the process difficult (Meadows 1993). They, however, will need added help and guidance to get it all together. It is at the point when it all comes together that learning is achieved and so the emphasis ought to be on monitoring the effectiveness of the process. If the process is effective, 'outcomes' will follow.

For convenience, above, I split the parts of the process into six: observation, memory, speculation, experiment, confirmation and acceptance. These are not sequential but componential. They are, one might say, the ingredient jars from which, with a measure of one and a measure of others, the business of concocting a thought is made up. The application of good detective work comes into its own as a means of working out which aspects are most in need of such fostering. If a pupil is precluded from dipping into any of the jars – say, by reason of poor short-term memory mechanisms – then it will be this aspect that will need nurturing and adapting. No amount of repetition of an action will, of itself, achieve a commitment to memory if the ground is not prepared to receive it. Some alteration in the strategic approach to the manner in which information is given will be necessary, some thoughtful interference on the part of a teacher to prevent the whole thought process from foundering from lack of an ingredient. I shall consider each ingredient in the order given above.

OBSERVATION

It is perhaps more usual to start a discussion on the thinking process in learning by invoking the term 'attention' (or perhaps 'concentration'). There are discussions in the literature about severe difficulties, on the need for a pupil to pay attention before there can be any intake of information (Evans 1986; Ouvry 1987); and, on the surface, that seems self-evident. Teachers are rightly concerned that their pupils 'pay attention and concentrate'. But attention is more than simply and apparently looking in the right direction. As we discussed when considering language and metaphor, the teacher's instruction to the pupil to 'pay attention' is too often monitored simply by trying to ensure that the pupil has eyes turned towards the desired focus, the ears are apparently pricked, and that is all. The real test of effectiveness, however, as far as any thought process is concerned, is whether there is any purpose behind the eyes, whether anything is going on in the mind as a result of pricking ears. The term 'observation' is being used here to indicate 'attention to a purpose'. Before attention can be engaged, the pupil must share with the adult the knowledge of what to look for or to listen out for; and that, as we saw when discussing detective work, is the essence of observation. In monitoring this, the teacher must bear in mind not only that the eyes are in the right direction but that the brain is able to switch on the process of making some use of the intake of the optic nerve and the sounds that are entering the ears or, in the case of severe sensory impairment, by any pathway that is potentially open.

MEMORY

Memory is an essential partner to the capacity to observe. Functionally, however, 'memory' is a term for at least two main component actions: *committing to* and *retrieval from*. Putting it simply: there cannot be a memory of an event unless there is a place to store the information and a memory is of no use if it cannot bring the event back into the conscious mind at some stage. We can go further. We can also assert that memory is crucial in deciding upon the uniqueness of any experience we may encounter. We search our memory and we say with certainty, 'I've never seen you before in my life!'. So reliably accepted is this aspect of memory that its malfunctioning is a major source of scary melodramas wherein the protagonist is tricked into believing that there has been a memory loss and that he or she really was present at some personally disastrous event (Meadows 1993, p.39).

In *committing* to memory, however, a pupil can only commit the sense he or she has made of the observation that preceded it. A memory cannot be stored in any form other than that which is understood at the committal. Of course, it can be modified on *recall* – and, in fact, that is what happens all the time. We commit a telephone number to memory and then, later, attempt to call it up. It is not our friend who answers. It is a wrong number although it is accurately a memory recall. We therefore have to adjust what we memorised – probably by realising that we had two numbers in the series reversed. We then have to commit the correct sequence to memory, probably reinforced in our understanding by the memory of having had it wrongly memorised before and of the process that corrected it. In this way committal and recall interact and learning takes place. There is considerable debate about and research on what causes memory to happen. It seems certain that it is a factor of interactions of synaptic connections across the brain and there is not a specific part that can be termed 'the memory' – although sub-functions of memorising, for example, short-term recall, can be shown to be affected by specific damage to brain areas (Obler and Gjerlow 1999).

There is also the brain activity known as *motor memory* which becomes established for regular use without it needing evaluative recall. Because it needs no evaluation, it can be said to occasion action without thinking. It is extremely useful in energy saving – we duck our heads entering a low doorway which we traverse habitually, thus saving the necessity of working out the space involved and the expending of explosive energy in our frustration at hitting our head painfully when we get it wrong. This type of memory can be, and indeed is, *trained*, both in social contexts – for example in the art of eating with knife and fork or in driving a motor vehicle – and in circumstances wherein physical performance is desired – for example in mastery of a musical instrument or specific body co-ordination in a sport. It can also be trained by methods of behaviour modification, a technique demonstrated by Pavlov's dog and the programmes that have followed it (Nmeroff and Karoly 1991). As a technique it is completely neutral; that is, it can be adapted for purposes of good – for example in the drills that are compulsory for recruits in emergency services that free the minds engaged in action to think of more than the handling of equipment – or less desirable – for instance, in inculcating crowd reactions to slogans or visual stimuli at the mercy of dictatorial politicians. The accompanying circumstances, variously classified as modification by contingent reinforcement or aversion, can be far more subtle than the often assumed (and crude) giving of a sweet following an approved action by the subject or administering something unpleasant following one that is disapproved. There are many subtle ways of bringing pressure on subjects, through motor memory, to act without thinking. There is a very real danger, therefore, that if a teacher relies on judging the educational progress of a pupil with severe difficulties purely and simply on performance, the results might have been obtained by programmes that preclude thought altogether. For this reason, to ensure that thinking is present, staff need to maintain a critical awareness of the process before evaluating the outcomes.

Such motor memory, however, is not a main focus in this section. It is, rather, the *active* processing both into and out of memory that is important. Where the difficulties faced are causing pupils to demonstrate confused *active memory* traces, then the exact nature of this particular problem, whether it is with commitment or retrieval, must be examined. These facets will be vital for the next focus of our own thinking in this chapter.

SPECULATION

Speculation is used here to indicate a function of what psychologists term working memory. Retrieval must be to some purpose; we do not generally use memory as a sort of family photo album, simply to recall past events for the purpose of enjoyment at leisure. Memory, in the thought process, allows us to reference back to experience (see Chapter 1) and gives our life a continuity. We live, in our thoughts, in a state of 'I wonder what would happen if...', 'What was it that I read about...?', and so on. We have to compare memory traces for possible solutions to everyday problems – say, how to move the car out of a tight parking space – equally with abstract ideas about whether whisky is a better drink than pineapple juice. In other words, we operate both pragmatically and poetically and have done so since birth. People differ in the degree to which they veer more to one end or the other of such a spectrum; but they operate somewhere along it. Thinking requires this constant, if not always overtly conscious, looking for the possibilities. We speculate to accumulate ideas which, in turn, will generate new ideas, and so on. Again, this speculation may occur as a factor of inner speech (see Chapter 4) the internal dialogue in our own minds, through language, which allows us to say out loud, when speculation has crystallised to some degree: 'I have an idea!'

When an adult refers to some pupils with difficulties and says, 'They have no idea', they may be speaking the literal truth. If the capacity for *speculation* is impaired the result is that much of the learning process fails to occur. One of the least developmental aspects of some severe difficulty states, for example, is the repetitive behaviour that has the pupil in its grip, the so-called *obsessions* (Waterhouse 2000). Even when such actions cause the pupil to perform in a way pleasing to staff – say producing perfect photographic drawings – there is room for some detective work to determine whether any speculation has illuminated the process.

EXPERIMENT, CONFIRMATION AND ACCEPTANCE

Experiment (both in the mind and in the physical world) is the natural next step from speculation (see Chapter 2). It is the step of 'I wonder what would happen if… Well then, let's see'. It has its dangers. One of the most important lessons that young children have to absorb is when it is safe and socially acceptable to carry out physical experiments and when they must be confined to the mind. The speculation/experiment aspect of thinking is probably the most tested in psychology because some of the strategies used to tease out some apparent answer to the 'Let's see' can be made quite transparent in a psychometric situation. Whether such test result gives the whole picture of the inner process in the pupil is open to doubt, but it is still most useful to a teacher to know how pupils set about this aspect of thinking.

Confirmation is used here to signify that to a given speculation a consequence has appeared. Note that in the process of learning the pupil does not have to realise any single particular consequence as being necessary in the sense that confirming a scientific experiment is to prove an hypothesis. Here I mean, simply, that there is a linked connection with the original 'Why?' that is experienced and passed back into memory for future use, for future speculation and for future refinement. Thus thinking progresses. As an illustration of what is meant, take the infant who goes to push her hand through the bars of an electric fire. The result of the experiment is likely to be finding herself pulled away from the vicinity somewhat roughly by a momentarily distraught parent and subjected to most emphatic and proscriptive language. She has, from the event, learned that a hand thrust forward towards that piece of furniture brings unpleasant and frightening results. That is the confirmation of her speculative action. What she has not learned, however, is that fire bars burn. She has, quite properly, been safely prevented from learning that result of her immediate speculation. Learning that fire bars burn will require a different social context and a carefully structured methodology of instruction. When observing the thought process of pupils in severe difficulties, it is important to attempt to tease out what, to each of them, is the confirmation of any self-generated action that may be passed back into memory. In evaluating processes, therefore, it is important to record not what the adult understands of a circumstance – that fire bars burn, for example – but rather what the pupil in difficulties has been likely to understand from the circumstances of an *experimentation*. What the pupil understands will be what the pupil has passed into memory (*acceptance*) for future use. This is not to say that what adults know from their own experience and memory is unimportant. That would be manifest nonsense. The result of an adult's previous confirmation and acceptance is, of itself, the basis of bringing up a child. If the hand is saved from the fire, then that is a necessary lesson, whatever the mechanics in the mind of the child. There is a need for a teacher to consider carefully precisely what the pupil has been able to pass into memory, what he or she has learned.

Implications for teaching

The mechanism

A teacher's task is to generate thinking as the vehicle for education. It is not to inculcate facts *per se*, nor is it to control a pupil's actions *per se*. Both acquisition of facts and self-control will happen the more certainly and the more profitably if the prime focus is always upon the generation of thought in the pupil.

There is a fundamental difference between the performance of a task and the *thoughtful* performance of a task. To perform a task, all that is needed is a certain motor competence and the ability to imitate. Such actions, however, apart from those wherein motor memory is the objective (such as, for example, taking a spoon to the mouth to feed) will not be useful unless they have a thoughtful element. It is this thoughtful element which has to be stored in memory if it is ever to be useful in the progressive accumulation of what is generally termed 'learning'.

Teachers must take care, therefore, that when they are setting tasks for pupils they also make explicit the factors which are crucial for the thought process that goes along with that task. At its simplest this means attempting always to give reasons within a pupil's comprehension for any task set. Pupils should not be seen going through tasks on the table in front of them, the purpose of which clearly escapes them. Certainly the teacher can explain why they are doing the task. Indeed, the tasks often come out of the textbooks on cognitive development. The problem, for the pupil, however, is that he or she does not understand the point of the task being set and therefore cannot *think* about it.

To that end, it is useful to commence each task by telling the pupil, 'I am asking you to do this because...'. It is not a reason to neglect this respect for the pupils if the adult says, 'They won't understand if you do tell them'. The only true reply to such a remark is, 'They certainly won't if you don't!'. Pupils must interpret, with reason, what is going on.

Shotter (1978) succinctly puts his finger on the nub of the argument:

> Thus to qualify as an autonomous person, not reliant like a child upon others to complete and give meaning to one's actions, one must be able at some point in one's acting to stop and to deliberate, and, as a result, make clear to oneself (and/or to others) one's reason for so acting. (p.43)

He expands this later in the chapter in a way that further illustrates my argument. He is writing about a mother talking with her infant and the rewards she is apparently giving.

> If, for instance, every time he made a pointing-like movement he was given a reward, a sweet, say, or anything other than his mother attending to the object he was looking at (or in some contexts giving him it), then one may indeed increase the frequency of his pointing-like movements. But the infant could never possibly learn that such move-

ments were something that could be used, not for getting sweet rewards, but for the social purpose of directing someone else's attention. (p.57)

Similarly, all the individual exercises (or tasks) that are set before pupils in general, and especially before pupils who are said to have 'learning difficulties', will get nowhere unless the pupils are given, within those tasks, the wherewithal with which to think. However well constructed the programme is, beware if it leaves pupils with what amounts to a bag full of parts but with no plan as to how to assemble them.

ASSEMBLY INSTRUCTIONS!

Care has to be taken, therefore, to ensure that the manifest 'learning difficulties' that pupils show – no matter that psychometric testing has given them a low IQ – are not compounded and perpetuated because they are not given guidance on the *process* of thinking. The low scores on IQ tests point to the fact that the potential for thinking will need careful and skilful nurturing and such nurturing is the province, largely, of the trained and skilled teacher. They do not indicate that thinking is impossible. This gives to teachers both a challenge and an opportunity to work with imagination *from the inside out* (see Chapter 1). It takes a deal of thought on the part of those of us who are educators to imagine what it is like to have severe difficulties. By the very nature of our progress to qualifications we have exhibited our capacity to think for ourselves. The responsibility, in this instance, is to enter into the difficulties and think along with the pupil. The teacher needs to take every step of the *process* with the pupil. Targets for achievement should be set with more emphasis on the process than on the outcome, each step advancing the pupil's capacity for constructing patterns of thought. Links must be built and then made explicit in terms that the particular pupil can be helped to understand. The capacity for grasping each sequential step will depend on where the pupil stands in relation to the next three principles that we shall discuss.

Second principle

Making conscious sense of incoming stimuli

CONSCIOUSNESS AND CHOICE

The use of the term 'conscious' directly implies the exercise of comparison and, from comparison, the arrival at a *choice*.

Here we must first distinguish between two fundamentally opposed concepts which are all too often confused in the practice of education. If the development programme of a pupil calls for opportunities to exercise choice, it is often reported, for example in a review, that 'there are many occasions in the day when this is made available to that pupil, e.g. he (she) is given the opportunity at drinks time to *choose* between milk and orange juice'.

In the context of this discussion that is not what is indicated by the concept of 'choice'. It would be more accurate to say that a pupil presented with such an alternative, was required to exercise *selection*. Choice, as I use it in this book, is to be understood as a conscious decision based on evidence in the pupil's mind – to prefer one interpretation of a stimulus to the brain rather than any other. It is a factor in the process of thinking. In the case of milk versus orange juice, the pupil had not had the opportunity to exercise any significant degree of thinking. The options before her or him are scarcely mind engaging. Something would have been added if the reporter, in the review, also noted that there was a third option – to refuse either; but often this option is simply, and literally, not on the table.

The choice, in this scenario, had been made some time before the incident reported; probably by the teacher in the supermarket deciding between the various competing claims of pop drinks, flavoured milk, mineral water, apple juice and then opting for milk (semi-skimmed) and orange juice (natural pressed) as the correct, healthy alternatives for her class to drink. Many considerations may have rightly influenced *her* thinking process, from health to social acceptability. Once the decision had been made, however, the alternatives were already circumscribed by her decision; the pupil could only select. It is not surprising that pupils then contrive to knock over their milk, thus establishing that they can exercise choice by refusing to be confined by selectivity. They are, however, not given credit for exercising it.

This is not to argue that in everyday life we regularly prefer choice to selection. Everyday situations demand regular and even routine selection on the basis of past choices, which enable us to opt for certain clothes from the wardrobe, food, newspapers and ice-cream without a prolonged process in the mind. The underlying point remains, however: that the options available have been laid down by the ability to refine the memory of genuine choices somewhere along the way and thereby to bring into play learned ability to problem solve from experiences.

As Siegler (1996) writes:

> ...many choices are made not through any specific choice module, or rational consideration of advantages and disadvantages of alternative actions, but rather through the ongoing interaction of strategies, associative knowledge, and problem-solving experience. (p.15)

STRATEGIES AND PROBLEM SOLVING

Strategies, associative knowledge and problem-solving experience(s) are essentials in the thinking process and are needful in establishing the end-product of *learning*. To think effectively we have to bring together what we know about the problem before us, the direction in which we want to proceed and a strategy for setting about the task. (Newell 1977)

Obtaining new information from old, as the result of choice of an appropriate strategy, is the way that the brain makes sense of the incoming stimuli, be those stimuli physical, in the sense of excitation of the visual, aural or tactile pathways or mental, in the sense of a linguistic entry into the inner processes of the mind. Thinking is, therefore, a factor of growth. Growth in thinking is exemplified by the sophistication of the strategic options open to the developing brain of the thinker. We think in order to grow, intellectually, as we grow to think, in order to be more effective thinkers.

What may well be hampering pupils in difficulties with their learning is that their progress has been limited in the matter of their *conscious development* of strategies that would have led to growth. Realisation of this point gives a focus for seeking to teach *thinking strategies* as the context for transmitting facts and gives another means of evaluating progress to enhance performance indicators of programmes *per se*.

Implications for teaching

Making conscious sense of incoming stimuli

One of the disadvantages faced by pupils whose brain processes are at
odds with what is generally met with is that the world still expects them
to react as if they saw it as others see it and hear it as others hear it. What
the brain links together and can store in memory for every individual
pupil may be at odds with the assumptions of those around.

As an example, let us together look at a picture of London. The
incoming light waves to our visual cortex will be the same to within
minimal variations depending on the angle of our respective eyes. I shall
therefore conclude that you are seeing what I am seeing, and mostly that
will be a fair and usable assumption. I am expecting the photograph of
London to be a view of scenery within which may be buildings and
people, water or birds, red soldiers or blue policemen, taken perhaps
from an aircraft or from low to the ground. My expectation will predispose me to make sense of what is in front of me and I begin to talk to you
about an item within the frame. But supposing, for the sake of this
example, that you are locked into colour alone and see splodges of
white, green, red and blue with indeterminate boundaries. The picture
will be of no use to you in knowing anything about solid objects in
London, although in artistic terms the colours may convey much for
your memory about the essence of London in a manner similar to that in
which an Eric Coates musical 'London Suite' impinges on the ear. If,
then, we wish to hold an intelligent (that is, thoughtful) conversation
about London based on the photograph, we shall have to find some
common interpretation of what is in front of us; otherwise I shall be
shouting into a void and you will be wondering (if you even bother)
what I am babbling on about.

In like manner, the common ground of making conscious and shared
sense of the stimuli in a lesson has to be found. When it is not clearly
made, then difficulties for pupils are compounded. For example, it is not
uncommon for pupils in difficulties to fail to distinguish figure and
ground in a visual display. This is often nothing to do with eyesight but
is occasioned by an idiosyncratic expectation of what to look for. As we
have seen in a similar discussion (Chapter 4), we need to have some idea
what we are looking for in advance of being asked to see it.

MORE ON ATTENTION TO A PURPOSE

The skill of teaching in these circumstances is to define precisely what are the boundaries to set on the incoming stimuli – light or sound or feel. Too often this step is assumed; that is, we assume that pupils are seeing in the same way as the adults around and therefore have an already innate attention to what is in our minds. The first instruction of an activity may be 'Look!'. Yes, but to what end? Attention has to be delineated before it can be meaningfully applied by a pupil, and it has to be meaningful before the pupil can focus on the precise stimulus to be thought about.

There are various ways of helping the definition process. In the visual field, the simplest is pointing, both by the teacher and by the pupil copying the teacher. This must not be vague gesturing with the index finger. 'Pointing' in this context has to be precise and must clearly show exactly what limits, within the visual field, set the subject of concentration. If it is a cow in a field then it is the outline of the cow in detail that has to be traced if it is to be made clear that she is the important element and all the rest is 'field' in both the actual and the technical sense. There are more precise variations that can be made in order to focus visual attention on its intended target. These range from even simple masking and revealing tricks, using a cardboard frame for a picture and within it a closing masking board, rather like the effects of an *f* stop on a camera, to the sophisticated use of computer technology for manipulating photo-imagery within the screen in front of the pupil.

In the auditory field, however, it is sometimes much harder. In a noisy room there are sometimes too many sounds which, once we know the desired area of focus, we can eliminate from our conscious thoughts; but we do it from prior knowledge of what is expected. As we saw in Chapter 4, amid the hubbub of the railway station we listen to make out what the station announcer is saying because we have already perceived a need to go to the right platform to catch the next train to our intended destination. We know what we are listening out *for*. Pupils in learning difficulties are, generally, in no such happy position and when told to 'listen' may well hear only confused noise – until, that is, they have something to listen out for. It is a known trick of the brain that it gives preference to aural stimuli that match a pattern that has been laid down. That is the mechanism that, for example, allows us to hear a word in a foreign language amid what otherwise is a meaningless babble when we have been told to 'Listen for the word "*musée*"'. The same is true of pupils in a class. When prepared with the key words as the focus of attention in a lesson or part of a lesson, then that attention can be paid meaningfully. It is a mistake to think that it is somehow being soft on pupils if they are given the tools for the job! Inexperienced staff are occasionally misled by being told 'They won't bother to pay attention if they know it already!'. This is simply mistaken. They will not be able to pay attention if they do not know the direction of the teacher's intention. There can be no thinking unless there is conscious sense made of such incoming signals, and the teacher's task is to provide the clues for such conscious sense to occur.

As a precursor to thinking itself, therefore, it is necessary to train the pupil in using the basic tools of thinking. One of the things that psychometric test results tell the teacher is, as it were, the number and capacity of the tools that a pupil naturally carries in the brain. In other words, the sub-tests all discriminate between aspects of the thinking capacity for which 'tools' is a metaphor. This is a measure of actuality, not of potential. The challenge the teacher faces is to devise the means to maximise the pupil's use of what is there in order to achieve the most fulfilling result. The reports from the psychologist should point the teacher to the areas of operation in the pupil's intellect that are most useful so that there can be a positive, pupil specific incorporation of these as the entry point of any teaching approaches. For instance, such results should show whether the pupil is active more in the visual or more in the aural sphere of sensory intake; or, indeed, whether he or she uses both with equal effect.

CLUES FROM TOUCH AND TASTE

The one area that is sometimes given little attention in tests with pupils in severe difficulties is that of *touch*. Often, however, pupils are in a developmental stage where the awareness of tactile information is still of primary importance; that is, the sense has not yet been finally superseded by a reliance, as far as physically possible, on sight and vision. 'Touch' sense includes, for the purposes of this chapter, that of taste and smell. The role of touch seems to be one of integration in the brain –

part of curiosity and experiment, the function of which was discussed in Chapter 2. In developmental terms it is more 'primitive' than other senses, both as communication (comfort, feeding, social cohesion) and self-identity (space and focus). Its obvious presence as a factor in the behaviour of pupils with delayed or eccentric development is, therefore, a sign that their thinking may not yet be sufficiently integrated to cope with the processing of information solely presented in 'adult' form. Since it is adults who control most of their formal learning this should lead to a moment of caution in any teacher preparing for the delivery of a programme.

I am not arguing that a pupil who consistently puts all objects into the mouth should be allowed to do so for ever, on the grounds that no more can be expected because of the developmental level. Developmental levels are there to be developed! It is, however, a reminder that the individual stage in the thinking capacity needs to be considered and that the pupil should be helped to move onward into a more advanced learning pattern. The argument against constant tasting and smelling is not about its initial value in development, which is undoubted and common to all children, but that it can (as can all stages of development) become stuck in certain pupils and therefore unproductive. The best way to consider any pupil who is thus stuck is to seek to acknowledge that the mouthing and sniffing are valuable but that the useful information contained in this sense of touch is also capable of being gained by other learning links and more developed processing.

Even here caution must be exercised. Pupils are thrust into bewilderment by inconsistencies that arise, unless the teacher is in control of the approaches used. What distinguishes useful taste, which has to be encouraged as part of the learning process, from using the mouth in socially unacceptable ways? What is a pupil who is constantly told off for putting objects into the mouth to make of it if, one day, he or she is suddenly instructed to put a substance into the mouth in an exercise designed to teach concepts of taste itself – sweet, sour, salty, etc.?

TEACHING THE ANSWER FIRST

The safeguard against this potential confusion, as in all other thought instruction, is to teach the desired end before embarking on the process. Put more simply, this is the practice that we have already met (Chapter 4) of knowing the answer first.

Teaching the answer first should be what all teaching is about, because thereafter the concentration is upon the vital thinking skill of process. Proceeding in this way is a safeguard against a lesson which in effect catches pupils out failing to answer questions they are asked, rather than ensuring that they succeed in learning what is required and, more importantly, how to arrive at it. There will be no guarantee that the pupils will know what the purpose was in the teacher's mind in asking the question. It is more profitable by far for the pupils to ensure that they will have the right answer at once by giving it to them and then exploring together the numerous ways in which that answer can be arrived at. In the matter of thinking, travelling excitedly is more beneficial than arriving.

Nor does this concentration on process work against the principal principle of *exploration*, wherein the pupil is seeking answers for himself or herself. In fact its effect is quite the opposite. By enabling the pupil to experience 'how to think', the teacher is opening up an understanding of how to explore. Exploration, after all, and as we saw in Chapter 2, springs from an inner voice saying 'What would happen if...?' which, in essence, generates the same thought process as the teacher's question, 'Now, how do we come at that answer?'.

Third principle

Thinking in a social and cultural context

A SOCIAL PHENOMENON

Thinking is a social phenomenon in the same way that language was seen as a social phenomenon. It takes place as a means of enabling us to exist with others, in family, in classroom, in business and in all other social groups of which we may be a part. While to be competent at thinking for ourselves is a definition of maturity, and while there is a very real sense in which our thoughts are private in origin, nevertheless the context for our ideas is the society in which we live and move

(Meadows 1993). That being so, our strategies closely relate to the structures in which that society construes the process and the ends to which it turns our thoughts. Young pupils have to bring into play (both literally and metaphorically) a knowledge of the norms of the society and the culture in which learning is taking place if they are to succeed in any formal learning that is evaluated within that society. Part of the skill of being a 'thinker' lies in being able to express the outcome of one's thoughts in the manner that the immediate society requires (Wood 1986). At the same time, being thought 'stupid' is rarely so much a clinical judgement of intelligence *per se* as a value judgement on a lack of social perception as viewed by a particular group at a particular time.

There is always a real danger that a group will ignore the thought process behind manifestations of ideas that are not expressed in ways with which the individuals are familiar. Cole *et al.* (1971), in a pioneering study among the Kpelle in Liberia, demonstrated clearly both the universality of efficient mental processes (there is no such phenomenon as superior *racial* intelligence) and the importance of examining thinking within its cultural and social contexts. What may be an effective thinking outcome in London or New York, if exported to the circumstances of the Kpelle, might be thought by them to be very stupid indeed – and, objectively valued, probably would be. The basic sequences of the mental process, however, would be exactly the same: only the metaphors would be different. This is partly because our thoughts work with the meanings that we have familiarly acquired and those meanings are couched in the semantics of our culture.

One of the lessons to be learned is that it is not sufficient to work on the mechanisms of thinking in those pupils with severe difficulties without also both being sensitive to cultural circumstances (ethnic origins, family pattern, etc.) and working to enable pupils to gain an appreciation of cultural meaning. It will not help pupils with severe difficulties to inculcate into them performances which have no context, however 'clever' those performances might seem. Thought has to be given to the purpose of any performance. For example, what do the pupils think they are doing when they perform a play or sing in public? I do not ask 'What are they told they are doing?' but ask staff to consider what inner understanding has come as a result of their thoughts.

Teaching pupils to think is not enough. It must also be a matter of teaching them to use their thinking processes in an appropriate context.

Implications for teaching

Thinking in a social and cultural context

The social order depends on shared thought and certain shared conclusions; not only for rules and laws but for shared certainties of conduct and morality that can be assumed. It would be tedious in the extreme if one had to rethink every social convention every time one needed to use it with another person. These conventions have been thought through and their cultural thought history is passed on, casually, to children as a matter of course. Therefore, when a pupil has missed out on any of the developmental stages in which this has normally accrued, there is a problem. Our social thinking relies on our being able to 'get into the mind' of the person with whom we are interacting and therefore it is necessary to understand not only how we ourselves think but the general rules of thought by which others also operate.

THEORY OF MIND

To do this we must have access to what is known to philosophy and psychology as a *theory of mind*. (Whiten 1991). Put simply, this means that for me to exercise the *theory of mind* I have to be able to work out in *my* mind how you will interpret in *your* mind any action I take. I have to be capable of seeing things from the other person's point of view (Wellman 1990). This involves my being able to use the language in my own mind (inner speech) to explain what is going on (Dunn 1991), first to myself and then by finding a means of communicating it when necessary to another person. There is evidence that young children, from a very early age of development, have the capacity to understand that the mind of another has its own independent feelings and, therefore, can modify their actions accordingly. In this sense, as in all matters of thinking, the potential of a theory of mind comes before the capacity fully to express it. The ability to work with another's mind and enter into the thinking of another person is refined and developed in increasingly complex linguistic exchanges, mainly through the process known as 'discourse' (Hickmann 1995).

DISCOURSE

For our purposes in this chapter, *discourse* can be defined as the means of forming joint thinking strategies about social situations. Thinking is going on at all times, every day, in all situations, whether to ourselves or with others, whether about a set problem or simply about the casual posers that merely living with others creates.

Thinking in this all-embracing sense has been developing in children from birth and its precise curricular application is generally what the teacher is concerned with. This cannot be assumed for pupils with severe learning difficulties. There is a danger, for the pupils with whom we are concerned, that if exercises to develop cognitive skills are confined simply to table-top activities, then the result will not be a pupil capable of thinking. The result will be a pupil capable of performing the exercises set. With care in the planning, of course, the exercises may build into a fair approximation of useful processes in specific circumstances, but the broad, balanced and appropriate education intended for the pupils will still lack a dimension. To appreciate this point, simply and intently observe pupils with difficulties in their normal classroom surroundings. The body language will tell you that, for much of the time, they are bewildered. They are not part of the 'thinking club' of which all the clued-up adults around and, in inclusive classes, most of their peers as well are paid-up members. Because one of the characteristics of severe learning difficulty is a tardiness in the process of *generalisation*, teachers cannot assume that one specific thinking task will spill over into a thinking strategy for use in social situations divorced from the context of the exercise – unless, that is, specific links are made as part of the day-to-day classroom practice.

Perhaps this is, in essence, the summation of the whole task for the teacher: to ensure that thinking is so much an explicit part of each day that pupils practise the art extensively to make up for what has not adequately happened developmentally. By 'explicit' I mean making it a daily habit to employ the technique of discourse, taking pupils into the confidence of the adults around and encouraging them to reciprocate – that is, explaining everything as it goes along. This gives a functional context for the commentary which we have considered both in Chapter 2 and Chapter 4. Teachers must respect the potential of pupils with difficulties to be adult thinkers and let them in on the secrets, or they never will be.

Fourth principle

Thinking and language: two sides of the same coin

THE LANGUAGE OF THOUGHT

Passing on the cultural inheritance of the elder to the younger, then, is an educator's professional task. This is done in small part by other means, such as by example to be imitated, but largely it is through tapping into the language of thought.

So much has been said already about the importance of language and of the way language, and meaning to be found through language, permeates the thinking process, that little remains to be added here. Nevertheless it is important to state it as a principle lest, in talking about special educational needs, consideration of the link is overlooked. For example, when considering a programme for a pupil with severe diffi-culties who is apparently struggling with the development of language, it has to be accepted that the strategies of thinking will be only as effective as the language constructs can carry. A pupil who has not yet the linguistic means to ask 'Why?' cannot be expected to exercise *specu-lation*: and without speculation it is unlikely that the pupil will be able to learn in a situation when left to himself or herself (see Second principle above, and the grammatical development stages in the Appendix).

Pupils will only be able to make sense of incoming stimuli within their language potential. Realisation of this can be useful in two ways. It will enable teachers to make educated guesses about what might be troubling pupils who seem to be disturbed by incoming stimuli – why, for example, certain tasks bring on tantrums. The pupil is simply unable to fit them into the language framework of meaning and thus is put into a state of panic. Equally important, it will signify that pupils who *do* appear to be able to make sense of these stimuli, but do not have speech, have an inner-language potential in excess of what they may be able to express. They will need to be given the words or signs with which to enter into a discourse with their thoughts.

Implications for teaching

Thinking with language

We have seen how the language of commentary on what is going on is a teaching tool to be developed for use in the classroom. There is, however, a more direct and directive aspect of the language of thought. Much of it takes place, ordinarily, as inner speech. For some pupils, however, it is not only necessary for the teacher to share the language of what is being processed in her or his mind but it is also necessary to put words directly into the minds of pupils and teach them how to use them. Just as mere exercises will not of themselves generalise in the pupils nor will the language of thought, however much the teacher hits the right note and makes explicit what she or he is doing. Pupils have to be given both instruction and permission to use inner speech.

Again the teacher can use the strategy of permitting the pupil to use specific words to make them personal. The best teaching always does this – gives to pupils the words by which to articulate their thoughts. While it is often the case that it is teacher's voice that is important – 'Be quiet and listen to me' – there should always be the opportunity for the instruction 'Be quiet and listen to yourself'. Otherwise, pupils will never learn to use their own voices in the context of being a *thinker.*

The idea of 'giving permission' and 'respect' go hand in hand. Teachers need to conceive of lessons in terms of opening up their minds to the minds of pupils; the more so when the pupil has profound difficulties. The language needs to be crafted in a form that is within the boundaries of, but pushing the boundaries of, what the pupil can process linguistically, but must contain all the relevant information for a thought process. For example, 'You may say to yourself, "This is the same thinking we did yesterday when we sorted blocks into groups of four; only now I'm doing it for real with biscuits for the others and myself"'. This says to the pupil that he or she is in the same league as the teacher; not as far up the league, maybe, but the same league nevertheless and using the same brain work. It also says to the teacher that he or she is using the same basic *process* as the pupil, albeit with more development. It is both a cultural and a linguistic sharing of respect.

There are two further particulars of language and thinking that a teacher has to bear in mind. Both have been partially dealt with in

Chapter 4 but may require reiteration in the context of the teaching of thinking skills.

STAGES IN THE DEVELOPMENT OF THINKING

First, consideration must be given to the natural way in which a pupil thinks. Those whose development has been less speedy than many may be using a form of thinking that is taken for granted in very young children but becomes squeezed out by what is generally promoted in schools as 'scientific method,' or 'thinking in exact quantifiable terminology'. Yet young children, and people of many cultures other than European, tend to base their thinking as they do their quest for meaning (which we met in Chapter 4) on *stories*. They reason in the context of a story and can thus come to the same end as many with abstract reasoning. Sometimes they can even be more penetrating in an answer than is the answer in the teacher's mind. This is the application in thought processes of what was discussed with reference to the idea of metaphor in Chapter 4. In the Ashaninca's language, in equatorial South America, the word *quinquithashiryaantsi*, 'to think', is closely linked in its root to words for 'remember', 'count' and 'tell a story', and forms an efficient semantic paradigm for the thought process itself. As we saw when discussing metaphor (Chapter 4), meaning is found by a process that goes from the greater to the more focused. In the same way teachers may, with profit to their pupils, exploit the potential for increasing the capacity to think by setting the desired process into the context of a story.

Here I am not meaning the sort of mnemonic that helped Guides and Scouts to tie a bowline knot – 'The rabbit comes out of the hole, round the trunk of the tree and back down the same hole' – although I have found myself retelling it to myself in the stress of needing to tie one first time in a gale at sea! Rather I mean the creation of apposite verbal pictures in which a thought process can be framed. If the pupil can be included as part of the story, so much the better. Many philosophers over the millennia have used story forms to stimulate thought, from Aesop, via Socrates, to the Humanists at the start of modern times. The effect of stories is not to give answers but to stimulate creative thought within which an answer can be tested out. Stories trust the listener to develop what is there; they do not confine themselves to definitive answers. Pupils with severe learning difficulties need such trust and respect. They cannot develop thought processes worth having if no one lets them develop them.

Too often children are told 'Think! Think!' without ever being given a notion of what that command means. The teacher approaching a common task with a story is, in fact, saying to the pupils, 'Let us together see if we can think about this. Let us tell a story about it. Let us suppose …'. It is a mistake to assume that pupils, as is sometimes said, need everything made concrete and practical. There is truth in the assertion, of course, because they do, on the whole, absorb lessons better when those lessons are 'practical'. But to construct lessons only in the world of the concrete is to leave them sadly lacking in necessary mind skills. The real need is for the concrete examples to be set clearly within the broader potential of supposition and story.

DEFINE

It is important to remember that the exact contextual meaning of some words must be defined or the pupils will be unable to think appropriately with them. These are special cases of having to define at the outset what is in the mind of the adult so that the pupil can understand what is going on in there. Possibly the most varied illustration of this phenomenon (but there are many) is the adjustment required in the meaning of the word 'more'.

Consider these sentences.

Do you want some more?

I have never seen you more excited, Rajinder!

Put down two cubes; now put down two more.

Four is more than three.

Four is one more than three.

There are more apples in the bag than pears.

The more the merrier!

Who has more cubes – you or Johnny?

Clearly in each instance the idea of *increase* is present, but how the increase notion is applied varies considerably. Take the last sentence as it is used in the following scenario. Teacher gives Johnny a pile of cubes and gives a smaller pile of cubes to Marva; then asks Marva, 'Who has more cubes – you or Johnny?' Marva points to herself! Clearly she has had an increase in her cubes – from nothing in front of her to a pile. But of course it is not the concept of absolute increase that was in the teacher's mind but comparative increase. How was Marva to know that?

The 'increase' aspect, although intrinsic, was incidental to the task in hand. If Marva was in severe difficulties already, then these would be compounded not by her low IQ but by the lack of clear thought lines, and she had not been provided with them.

It ought now to be quite easy for any adult to sketch out scenarios for any of the above sentences wherein similar confusions could reign if the pupil was not clear about which thought process to use. Tell a story about it!

And what do you make of the following riddle? 'If numbers make you numb, what do more numbers make you?'

UNSTICKING THE SYSTEMS

As we saw in Chapter 4, the capacity to play with language depends on the thinking–linking process of experimenting and playing with the meanings possible within sound patterns. The fact that many pupils with profound learning difficulties appear not to be able to play with even simple language is partly because they may not have been helped to move among varied thinking processes and are, literally, stuck fast with only one system. Selecting appropriate thinking strategies for contexts is one of the more important skills that is a function of education and the appropriate inner speech should be modelled so that the pupil has a chance to practice *thinking about thinking.*

Fifth principle

A person must be able to think about thinking

THOUGHT DEALS BOTH WITH ACTUALITY AND WITH POSSIBILITY

To be an effective thinker anyone must build up a picture of herself or himself as 'a cognitive person' (Meadows 1993, p.79). From a very early age children can be heard to say, 'I *think*...' and must mean something by it. It must be the result of awareness of something that they feel is going on in the mind (Fodor 1994).

To control thought we must be aware of thinking; to develop strategies for effective memory we must be aware of what it is to remember and to forget; to plan effectively we must know how to evaluate future possibilities against our knowledge of past realities.

When children come, very early, to a realisation of themselves as *thinkers*, they may not yet have the language capacity to explain what they are doing when they are 'thinking' but all the signs tell us that they realise that there is an internal process of their mind which they control for themselves. They can be heard to state quite firmly, when interrupted, 'No! I'm thinking'. This means something; it is not simply a copy of what they may have heard an adult say, because it is not context bound, as many imitated social phrases tend to be. The limits of context-bound copying is the subject of many a story of the child who enunciates very clearly a remembered phrase but to the wrong person. By contrast, children use the 'thinking' phrase randomly in connection with an inner and developing awareness of their speculative powers and, indeed, a realisation that it takes time and personal space. One of the biggest mistakes in educating pupils with severe learning difficulties is an insistence that they must be 'on task' all the time – busy. Now it is true that the brain needs to be active and a somnolent mind will not learn very much; but, equally, there has to be thinking going on and thinking needs time. Some gazing around the room or looking at the ceiling or even closing of the eyes might be indicative of a stubborn determination to be idle, but then it might be a sign of wrestling with a thought. And think, for a moment, how much thoughtful planning is involved in being purposefully idle! Too much activity, without a pupil having the chance to practice thinking, will not solve any of life's problems.

As the corollary holds, thinking is not only our means of existing in the present by reference to the past but also of projecting into the future. Thought is necessary to place us in continuous time, as opposed to our being locked permanently in present time. The severe difficulties faced by some pupils may appear to lock them into present time so that they only 'project', as a strictly timetabled habit, into a grasp of what routinely 'happens next' or perhaps into a memory of an event triggered by a sound or the sight of a photograph. That, however, may be enough of a foothold to spread the excitement of possibility, if nurtured carefully by good teaching. And to possible approaches to stimulating thinking we shall now turn.

Implications for teaching

Thought: actuality and possibility

The final consideration for a teacher in teaching about thinking is to realise that if a pupil can be helped to understand the structure of thinking, then that pupil has a better access both to memory and to planning. One of the worst feelings that arises when the brain is malfunctioning in some way is the feeling of being trapped in the present and being unable to think one's way out of it. It is one of the symptoms of depressive illnesses. The past is a closed book of vague memories that cannot be reopened or a series of snapshots with no connectivity. The future cannot exist. Projection into the future needs imagination, and imagination is a factor of thought.

Teaching thinking skills, therefore, is fundamental to allowing a pupil a more satisfying life, at even the most apparently basic level. The apparent basic level may be, simply but stultifyingly, a result of not being educated into the capacity to think a way out!

Connectivity

At the simplest level it may be a matter of ensuring that there are clues around that show how to link the present to the past and to the future: that enable the pupil to make connections. For example, one of the best uses of video recordings of any activity with a class is to reactivate the past actions for pupils in the context of changing the way language is used. There is a different linguistic register in going over old events which is a vehicle for memory and which relies on mental recall of the scenes in question. For pupils in difficulties, the exact stimulus of 'what happened' may be needed in order for recall to be activated; but the purpose of the exercise is more than simply the equivalent of looking at holiday snaps. It is to generate, in retrospect, the very same language of thinking that was used at the time but to restage it in the present and evaluate it.[2] 'Look! When I sat there crying I was unhappy. Look! When I ran up to the ice-cream van I was laughing.'

The same thoughtful function is required to project into possible future events from what is happening in the present. There is a loop effect from an evoked memory of the past, through a consolidation in present time and into consideration of what might happen. The simplest loop device is the timetable. It encapsulates what is about to happen today on the basis of a recall of what happened last week. Discourse about the timetable for the day brings together (linguistically) all the elements in thinking about the loop and can give the pupils practice, at the moment of the chat, in both how to think into the past and how to think into the future. Once again, as in previous aspects of thought, the role of the teacher is to make things explicit, demonstrating how links are thoughtfully made from experience into expectation.

There are dangers. The loop can be a source of fright as well as of confidence. Pupils with emotionally bad experiences of the past, for example a dog leaping at their wheelchairs in a shopping mall, may simply project any awakened memory of that time into all proposals for a second walk into the mall unless the whole process of 'thinking it through' has been undertaken. As we shall see in Chapter 6, often the reason for behaviour that is difficult to handle is that there is no thought involved in it. It is simply arising out of the emotions (fear, panic, sexual drive, hunger, affection or deviant versions thereof) and is properly called 'thoughtless'. There is absolutely no point in merely attempting to correct such behaviour by telling pupils to 'think' unless they have been educated into and practised in the thinking process itself.

One of the disadvantages of being trapped into an emotion is that the brain then freezes out rational thought and the mind loses balance. Preserving balance for pupils is of the utmost importance. It is a little-realised aspect of a 'broad and balanced' curriculum.

It is always worth remembering that balance involves keeping a judicious grasp of two sides to every question, two aspects to every thought. Staff and pupils alike need to have constantly in mind that for every speculation 'Supposing it does' there is an equal and opposite logical thought 'Supposing it doesn't'. 'Supposing that dog jumps up at me', set against 'supposing that dog doesn't'. To assuage panic and its resultant tension-behaviour, a pupil with learning difficulties has to be helped to the thought that in every apprehension of an event as yet unreached there is a strong possibility that it may not happen.

Notes

1 The importance of striving to generate thinking pupils as the prime focus of education has been the subject of much study. The importance of an understanding of process to achieve this aim has generated many books and led to insightful and stimulating ideas. I suggest below four (comparatively) recent and readable books for those excited by thinking and the opportunity to work in dialogue with the minds of pupils.

2 There is an important psycholinguistic phenomenon at work here. Videotaping not only records factually what happened but it also re-presents it at a later time to the contemplation of the mind in a way that was not possible while the action was being factually experienced. The ready accessibility of the videotape recorder has provided teachers with a means of guiding pupils through the language of contemplation in a way that still photographs did not fully manage. Drawing upon ideas of what happened to spectators at a play in a theatre, Britton (1970) pointed out the difference between the language generating thoughts during an event when we are participating in parts of the action and the language that generates our 'going over the event in our mind' at a later date. A notable contrast between the language employed by a 'participant' and that employed by a 'spectator' is that the latter is more evaluative, more judgemental. It allows for self-evaluation, the increase of memory traces and a chance to consider those around the action who might have been outside our vision during it. In this it helps awareness of a *theory of mind*. It also can act as a practice session for the 'video' we all play when we privately go over things in our minds. It is worth remembering that pupils with difficulties in learning and in using language have to be helped to deal with themselves, to use their thinking when the adults are not around.

Further reading and study

For thinking and the teacher's role in stimulating it

Fisher, R. (1990) *Teaching Children to Think*. Hemel Hempstead: Simon & Schuster Education.

Meadows, S. (1993) *The Child as Thinker: the Development and Acquisition of Cognition in Childhood*. London: Routledge.

Nelson, K. (1996) *Language in Cognitive Development: The Emergence of the Mediated Mind*. Cambridge: Cambridge University Press.

Wood, D. (1998) *How Children Think and Learn*. 2nd edn. Oxford: Blackwell.

CHAPTER 6

Behaviour

The interrelation between language, learning and behaviour.

(Beitchman *et al.* (1996), Preface, *Language, Learning and Behavior Disorders*).

In this chapter I shall discuss conduct in the sense of how pupils conduct themselves – which is the colloquial manner in which the term *behaviour* is used. I shall also explore the implications of altering such behaviour where that may be desirable. Discussion will be based on four *principles* and three *corollaries*. They are:

1. Behaviour is a neutral term for anything a person does.

   Corollary: It is the *action* that is the behaviour and the action that may occasion a problem. (Therefore, the term cannot properly apply to a person, as in the phrase 'He is a behaviour problem'.)

2. To be termed 'appropriate', behaviour should be considered against two questions:

   (a) Is the action socially appropriate in the relevant culture?

   (b) Is the action age appropriate?

3. For a pupil to be held responsible for a specific action, that pupil must be conscious of, and in control of, the origins of that action.

Corollary: For every behaviour under review the prime question to ask is, was there an *intention* to perpetrate that behaviour in order to cause the reaction that it reportedly occasioned in those around?

4. Any interpretation of the intention behind an action in a pupil must be consistent in all respects with the assessed *level of thinking* of which the pupil gives evidence.

    Corollary: The reverse also holds good: that if a pupil appears to have perpetrated a behaviour stemming from and requiring sophisticated thought, then that pupil should be presented with work that exercises the mind to that level of thinking.

First principle

Behaviour is anything a person does

COROLLARY: THE ACTION, NOT THE PERSON

If pupils are to be helped *from the inside* (see Chapter 1) they need to have the things they do analysed fairly. There is always a natural temptation when we are involved in someone else's behaviour – let us say being kicked – to let our natural reactions colour how we report the incident, first to ourselves and then to others. It is always as well to remember that the first report of any incident is always in our own inner speech; we 'have it in mind' before ever we report it in expressive language and so we have already put an interpretation upon it.

When the behaviour is a problem to us, we then may tend to see the whole pupil as the problem. At best, this militates against an understanding of, and thereafter an amelioration of, the behaviour itself and, at worst, results in behaviour on our own part which may of itself be inappropriate.

If we perceive a behaviour as causing a *problem*, the first action that is required is *problem analysis*.

PROBLEM ANALYSIS

In problem analysis we ask:

- Who has the problem with this behaviour?

- Is the problem one of management or one of communication?

- Is there a problem in our own reactions to the behaviour?

In a tense classroom situation, it may seem obvious who has the problem! The staff have the problem! But this may be too facile a view. The discussions concerning pupils once referred to as 'maladjusted' defined one sub-classification of the group as those pupils whose behaviour is as much a problem to themselves as it is to others (Laslett 1997). Although the subject of this book is pupils with generally more severe learning difficulties than that group, there always remains the possibility that the pupils themselves are conscious of a problem with their own behaviour in which they feel trapped. If they are not conscious of their own behaviour then that raises a different issue and we shall discuss the implications later in this chapter.

Because all noticeable behaviour is a public act, no participant can escape the context of social signals. All actions here discussed, therefore, have to be experienced in a *social context* to be a problem under this principle. How the pupil in question is acting and *re*-acting in general in a social context, is one of the essential clues to look for in problem analysis. If, for instance, the pupil acts and then seems bewildered and distressed by the result of the action, we must consider the possibility that he or she is, himself or herself, having a problem with the behaviour in question. It may be that the problem arises from an awareness of the social signals occasioned by the action (extreme displeasure voiced by the parent, for example) but the link between the rejection and the behaviour itself is not being made by the pupil concerned. Their bewilderment would be arising from imperfect *reasoning* which was briefly discussed in Chapter 5; but it still results in a problem for that pupil.

It may be that it is adults who find this particular behaviour to be a *problem*. It is then necessary to be clear whether, for any individual adult, the problem is:

- physical (for example, being kicked) and therefore one of physical management of a situation

- autonomic (for example, a personal, immediate and automatic revulsion at, let us say, spitting) which is personal, understandable but requires discussion to sort out who else might feel more able to deal with the situation

- temperamental (being personally irritated by the action, for example, 'I can't stand that constant drumming with his heels on the floor') which requires both understanding of the various reactions to the behaviour, on everyone's part, and suitable management strategies so that the member of staff can diffuse with honour the feelings generated while still helping the pupil become more socially integrated, or

- moralistic (the a priori belief that any such act is wrong *per se* and calls for punishment).

SOME WORDS ABOUT THE NOTION OF PUNISHMENT

The *moralistic* view of behaviour is, of itself, the hardest to manage; if only because it is, in itself, evidence of deep-seated social conditioning in the moraliser and, almost by definition, has moved beyond any complex analysis to simple and often simplistic reaction. Moral stances seldom come from entirely personal reasoning but are part of a specific religious or cultural upbringing. They rely on a code which was originally laid down for practical, historical and cultural reasons but was then handed down as a belief system. While philosophers, in striving for common understanding, debate ethics as a universal underpinning of all moral systems, most people behave more or less in accordance with precepts of a code, not worrying about its underlying validity (Warnock 1998). The function of problem analysis in response to any behaviour by a pupil is to isolate what is a reasoned reaction from what is a conditioned reaction brought about by a code. It may be that the resulting disapprobation remains the same; for there is nothing wrong with having a moral code. What will certainly be part of the reasoning, however, is the element of *punishment* such an action merits. For punishment, in all codes, is a fixed consequence of certain specified actions on the part of an individual under disapprobation, and a required reaction is laid down in parallel with the definition of the offence as it is perceived at the time in the social thinking of the society in which it occurs.

When we are interacting with pupils whose learning difficulties are severe, however, the problem with punishment is that its purpose is never entirely clear. Even in a society's code of law, it is a matter of debate whether required punishment is in place to reform the offender, to act as a dire warning to others or to inflict the retribution that the society feels is justified. This holds good for any society, be it a nation or a classroom. Once in place, the code is absolute and any breach of it requires that punishment ensues. This is defined as 'justice' or as 'fairness'. Justice is indifferent. The notion of 'fairness', therefore, sometimes overrides the notion of assessing each action in personal terms applicable differentially to different individuals, as in such a comment as 'It wouldn't be fair to the others if I let you get away with it'. All societies must have some form of code if they are to be regulated and cohesive and it is therefore natural to a society to assume punishment for breaches of that code so that good order may be preserved among its members. But is the code for general guidance or is it drawn up for rigid adherence?

The code of a classroom

How does consideration of society's need for a code enter into discussions over the education of pupils with severe difficulties?

First, it is important that any staff dealing with pupils who behave in ways that constitute a problem are aware of their own membership of a society that makes codified demands upon themselves. We all live under the law which will proscribe certain actions and lay down penalties for any violations.

Second, therefore, it needs to be recognised that the basic orientation towards the need for a code, and its inherent assumption of punishment for violation, is deep within the subconscious of all members within a society – teachers no less than judges. Discussions about the management of behaviour in the society of a classroom, especially a society embracing pupils in severe difficulties, needs to be open about this underlying feeling and to ask the question, ' Is it appropriate to be moralistic about any action or are there pertinent rational arguments that show a way forward more clearly?'.

It is, for example, of the utmost importance, if the educational objective for the pupil is to be towards altering certain behaviour, to ask, 'what is the purpose of this punishment?'. Which of three possibilities is intended? Is it directed at reform of the offender, as a warning to the rest of the group, or as retribution? These three questions are part of the necessary problem analysis.

PUNISHMENT TO CHANGE BEHAVIOUR

Punishment as a way of altering behaviour has been used in dealing with pupils with severe difficulties and to an extent is still considered. It is now mainly linked to one manifestation of the management technique of *behaviour modification* which was touched upon in Chapter 5. It is based on the underlying principle that all action is conditioned as a reaction either to pleasure or to pain.[1] By giving something pleasant to a pupil in conjunction with an approved action the adult will reinforce that behaviour and providing something unpleasant in conjunction with a disapproved action will diminish that action. This is directed at modifying the offence, thereby making the pupil fit for the society (however defined) of which he or she is a member.

The evidence, however, is that, as a means to reforming an offender punishment is seldom successful (Parker and Allerton 1962). In criminal studies, it becomes clear that the behaviour of many criminals is not *within* so much as *against* the code itself, and the unpleasant consequences of any challenge only reinforces that challenge. It is clear, in criminology studies and books on behaviour management in schools, that *reform* must be based on different premises from punishment (Scherer, Gersch and Fry 1990), and there is no reason to believe that the underlying principle should be any different for altering behaviours in children. It must be remembered that, unless the pupil can make a direct mental link between the intention of the act he or she committed in breach of any code and a corrective intention in any punishment meted out, there can be no learning taking place, only a conditioned reaction (Skinner 1972).

'I'M WARNING YOU!'

Punishment as a *warning* is still current in some people's educational thinking. What has to be taken into account in any analysis of this as a technique for managing pupil behaviour is the peculiar fascination that we all feel for seeing others in trouble. This seems to apply to pupils with apparent limited capacity for reasoning no less than the rest of us. The popularity of 'entertainments', from Tom and Jerry cartoons to chamber of horrors waxworks, are evidence that there is a deep-seated drive at work here. The danger of *open* punishment in any group where there are pupils with severe difficulties is that the circumstances may, indeed, be reinforcing this drive; even as the pupils may not have the capacity to conceive of its potential application to themselves or understand why it is being applied to the victim (Skinner 1972, p.288).

The ultimate sanction in the code of any group is to turn an offender away. A decision in favour of exclusion from a school also rids the institution of the need to even consider the behaviour further and in more depth. When it comes to a group in which the undesired behaviour arises in a pupil with severe difficulties and where the objective should be to help the pupil to alter the action by understanding of the root causes, it is unhelpful to turn the pupil out of the group in which such an understanding should be centred.

Sometimes, however, it is argued by adults that the non-social behaviour in question might influence other pupils to act in the same way – 'copy-cat' behaviour. Sometimes in an *inclusive* educational setting this is an expression of parental fears for their child mixing with the pupil with difficulties. These arguments are irrational. In an ordinary inclusive grouping, there would be no pupils who would be driven to behaviours outside the code unless they were in severe difficulties themselves. Again, mockery and bullying are themselves symptoms of perceived fears and uncertainties in the group rather than unilateral actions of one or two pupils. When they occur, it may well be a sign that it is the code itself that is geared more to ostracism than to inclusion.

THE CHILD IS NOT THE BEHAVIOUR

The safeguard against confusing management and punishment is, in all circumstances, to apply the corollary to this principle. Just as it is slack use of terminology to talk about a pupil as a *behaviour problem*, so it is slack talk to speak of *punishing a behaviour*, since a behaviour is an action and can feel neither pleasure nor pain. Behaviour is, I must repeat, of itself neutral. Punishment is always directed at a person. It is the pupil in the frame, not that pupil's actions. The more need, therefore, to analyse the behaviour to ascertain what it means for that individual pupil.

BEHAVIOUR AS COMMUNICATION

The possibility that a behaviour is a *communication* has always to be taken into account. Indeed, when any action (that is, any behaviour) is deliberately used as an item of communication – as in gesture, either 'natural' or in a recognised sign system – then it clearly fulfils this role. The problem (for analysis) arises when there is a difficulty in the communication system itself. This is obvious in speech, when the articulation is distorted, or in awkward physical co-ordination when the fine motor control necessary for signed communication is imprecise. In either case the meaning apparently intended by an action may be contrary to the end result. Similarly, in analysing the communicative element in other problem behaviours, therefore, it is necessary to ask: 'What was the intention behind this action and how did it become a *problem* rather than a *message?*'.

REACTIONS AND CHALLENGING BEHAVIOUR

The final consideration in problem analysis concerns reaction. This makes a necessary switch from the action of the pupil in focus to the reaction of the adults or pupils around.

Every behaviour has a consequence; it is a matter of determining whether the reaction of those around is likely to alter and improve the behaviour or to perpetuate and exacerbate it. Extreme actions (violence, for example) are now commonly referred to as *challenging behaviour* (Fleming and Kroese 1993), but the term itself requires some analysis. Where is the root of the challenge?

The use of the term as applied in analysis of behaviour appears to involve the notion that it is we, the adults around, who are challenged to find a profitable solution by the fact that we are witnessing the action. That is the most acceptable contextual meaning for the phrase. The challenge lies in the particular idiosyncrasy of the behaviour itself, and the reference in the use of the word in analysis is to intellectual exercises, to puzzles that we might undertake because we find them 'challenging' and thus their resolution stimulating.

The colloquial use of the word challenge, however, always implies the desire for a winning outcome, as in 'a sporting challenge'. In sport it carries with it an implied threat – ' I intend to prove to you that I am superior'. Accepting the challenge, in this sporting context, means that I, in my turn, am saying 'Come and prove it then, if you can!'.

Conflating these two quite distinct shades of meaning – the intellectual and the gladiatorial – can be very dangerous when applying the term to the behaviour of another person. Unless there is vigilance in monitoring the reactions of all concerned in the circumstances of behaviour that can be violent or emotionally stressful, it may not be the intellectual aspect of the situation that comes to the fore but the confrontational. If there is even a suspicion that we are being drawn into a reaction to the other person that says, 'Don't think you can get the better of me', then we are interpreting challenge in the gladiatorial way. There is immediate danger both to the pupil and to our own professional ability because, within education, it is never a matter of 'winning' against a pupil but of helping the development in each pupil. The usage of the phrase has, unfortunately, allowed some people to think in terms of conflicts, not in terms of solutions. Again, keeping the corollary to this principle always in mind is a necessary safeguard.

Implications for teaching

It is not at all easy, as a member of staff, to separate an actual disturbing behaviour from the feelings it engenders. When we are in the presence of a pupil with severe impairment the social balance is altered by the fact that it may not be possible for adjustments readily to be made, on both sides, nor a reasoned answer given to the question: 'Why did you do that?'. We saw in Chapter 4 that staff will encounter pupils who respond to being asked that question, if they have speech, with 'I don't know', and if they have no speech, with a body language equivalent. This response, in turn, sometimes leads the adult to the retort 'Of course you know!'. Such an exchange has all the makings of an escalating confrontational situation.

Stand back a moment, however, and observe such a situation developing. The adult has been angered and is displaying the body language of extreme suppressed irritation. The pupil is, almost certainly imperfectly, aware of these signs and possibly conscious, therefore, of having breached some code, but probably does not have a clear rational view of what caused his or her act. The pupil's body language is one of confusion and bewilderment. What answer is possible for such a pupil other than 'I don't know'? But it does not resolve the situation either for the adult or for the pupil.

There are two, more profitable, ways forward in such a stand-off, allowing that we all, at times of exasperation, will ask non-questions such as 'Why did you do it?' of pupils with difficulties.

The first approach is simply to assert that the behaviour has crossed the line of the acceptable code, without question. This can have two effects: it reinforces a firm boundary for the pupil and yet it continues to include the pupil within the social code of the peer group. An interesting example of this approach concerned a boy who was being moved, within an inclusive setting, from primary to secondary school. He had been disruptive in his last term in primary school and the messages being passed by staff across to their secondary school colleagues were full of gloom and doom. On his first day at the new school, in the dining hall, he came to the attention of the Special Educational Needs Co-ordinator (SENCO) who was on dinner duty. He was indulging in some unwanted and unpleasant food ritual. Fixing him with an authoritative stare, but in a voice that merely conveyed the necessary information, she said, 'We don't do that at this school'. The behaviour stopped, never to reappear. Having been given the code, he could establish a boundary within it.

The second approach, instead of asking the direct question of the pupil, is to join in the question with the pupil. 'Now, let's try to work out why you did that.' This approach assumes that pupils, especially those with language difficulties, need help to find the right words before they can ever explain their own actions. In this case, the adult's responsibility is to act, as it were, on both sides of the social situation simultaneously. This self-discipline of attempting to enter into any action of a pupil as much as possible *from the inside* is necessary as a safeguard against imputing motive to the pupil. There are myriad reasons possible for almost any item of behaviour. Most of them might reasonably and immediately be eliminated in any particular context as remote, but in every case there will remain more than one sensible, possible reason. Therefore, as a matter of professional practice, staff should set themselves the discipline of considering at least two possible antecedents for any act, positive or negative, which they witness, and suggest these to the pupil.

This forces consideration to focus upon the action in its immediate context.

I shall deal in more detail with alternative possibilities for behaviours under the Third principle below; but as an illustration at this point, take the behaviour of a pupil attempting to bite the teacher's arm. Is the pupil driven by a desire to take a purposeful lump out of the teacher, or to find anything reasonably accessible and plastic enough to act as a counter to intolerable toothache? And if, at this juncture, experienced readers are saying to themselves 'Come on! There are other reasons I know of that make children bite!' then my point is made. Any item of behaviour may have many potential antecedents. Simply pausing to find two possible reasons, even if one of them is of doubtful authenticity, disciplines the mind of the staff member to open up more than two which might be considered. In this there is a safeguard for pupil and staff member alike: to prevent 'knee jerk' as far as possible and to allow approaches to altering the behaviour to be based on rational thought, not on passionate reaction.

Staff reaction

Let us look at this matter also from inside the teacher, because the reaction of staff members may spring out of emotion rather than rationality. This is, in fact, the more common daily reaction of all of us to social behaviours in general, and is no surprise. The emotional reaction only becomes dangerous when it gets in the way of rationality in circumstances in which the member of staff has to interpret what is going on from both sides at once. When the other party is unable to put his or her side of a behaviour, through lack of a capacity for dialogue or from any other cause, then there is a professional imperative upon that staff member *not* to react emotively. This is easier said than done, that much must be acknowledged. We shall now look, therefore, at some strategies for easing the emotional strain and opening up the circumstances wherein rationality is more likely than not to be the reaction to any item of pupil behaviour.

First, then, in dealing with any behaviour that is at all challenging, discard the first reaction, whatever it is, and think of another – any other – quickly, and address that interpretation of the cause of the behaviour.

It may not prove to be the right one. That scarcely matters, because it is necessary, with any behaviour that causes some turmoil, to talk it through with a 'neutral' colleague as soon as possible afterwards and record its incidence and impact. Acting on the second reaction guarantees at least that some thinking has been forced into the situation and that the member of staff is unlikely, then, to act on a 'knee jerk'. This, simply, protects both parties. Emotional reaction to behaviour which challenges has been in years past a source of questionable treatment of those with mental impairment and a reason for questioning the legality of the actions of those in charge. Both parties need a safeguard from drifting into a danger area in human care and control. As a matter of generality, staff will find that their second thoughts enable them to take that split second to adjust and that they will feel the more content that they have handled situations without doing anything they might regret.

Having second thoughts in adverse circumstances is not easy, without practice. There is, therefore, a need to accustom staff to the principle during staff training and help each member to find his or her own technique for going into the 'second thought mode'. A useful starting point, as a training exercise, is to take any behaviours that staff find particularly stressful and emotionally challenging and to ask staff members to recall such a behaviour in themselves – no matter when, possibly as a child. In a trustful group, members may then be able to give a reason (as a mature adult) for what they were feeling at the time and for what triggered the behaviour. For many behaviour patterns – spitting, biting, kicking, running away, screaming, refusing to move in the supermarket, fear of dogs, sudden panic attacks, and others – there will be personal memories, since most people have exhibited versions of them. The memory, however, is not always pleasant, and confession is hard; therefore some care and gentleness is necessary in helping staff towards this technique of 'second thoughts'. Nevertheless, insight into oneself is the first step towards insight into a situation where one has to act on both sides and find explanations that help pupils.

Second, because the best form of dealing with any difficult situation is often to prevent it, there is a need to foster the circumstances in which creative and positive social behaviour can flourish. The analysis of positive behaviour is so much more healthy than simply planning to prevent adverse behaviour. For one thing, the emphasis is couched in the right language and leads thought into action in pursuit of the comfort and satisfaction of the pupils rather than, as unfortunately so often happens, to their containment. If the incident record sheets of a school consist only of a tick-list of all the possible adverse behaviours, however unlikely, that a pupil may perform, all the possible damage that might ensue and all the possible people who might have been hurt, then it forms a hope-less document. If there are no counter-incidents, positive behaviours, then the document is a charge sheet more than an educational aid. Of course there needs to be a detailed record of any adverse incident but there has to be room, in all the detail, for the record to show what was positive, what was simply human in all that was happening. Remember that it was an important point in the alertness of the detective (Chapter 3) to observe the normal that everyone else had ignored.

Positive approaches

What, then, are positive actions which may make pupils more comfortable with themselves and more socially able?

ALLOWING SPACE

One of the most insistent problems for pupils with severe difficulties is to find enough personal space. They are often, with the best of intentions, under *adult control* most of the time and intensively taught on the basis of constant adult attention. It can be a frustrating experience for both parties. While the management of the situation in the classroom may allow the adults to work on a rota system it does not allow the pupil to rotate between intensive help and periods of contemplation. If the pupil has no ready speech, and if there have been no 'personal choice' or 'social interaction' signals built into any communication system in which the pupil has been taught, then sheer frustration and the need for space may be behind such actions as kicking or spitting. In analysing behaviour as *communication*, therefore, one of the first questions to ask is whether the pupil has access to a shared and acceptable means of signalling the message 'For goodness' sake get away from me before I explode!'. If the answer, on analysis, is 'no', then the resulting explosive behaviour may be the communication.

It is shortsighted on the part of adults working with children in severe difficulties and without ready speech if they introduce a sign system or a rebus system that does not include *from the start* the means to express emotions, including frustration. To neglect the need for a pupil to communicate – 'You are getting on top of me', or 'I've a bad headache', or 'I find Carl fascinating' – and to assume that the only necessary words are such control communications as 'drink', 'biscuit' and 'toilet', is to create the circumstances in which behaviour-as-a-problem will surely arise.

Much anxiety is caused by indifference to personal space. Particularly when pupils are unable to establish social space for themselves, through immobility or lack of social awareness, they are likely to be crowded by other people; sometimes especially by those trying to help. Often it is the result of anxiety – keeping a pupil held fast by the hand lest something adverse (running away, attacking another pupil or whatever) is perpetrated. As containment it works most of the time but it has to be maintained constantly or the pupil may run off at the first slackening of the hand. We have to ask 'What is the pupil running from?' and then consider the possible answer that the pupil is running as a reaction to close confinement. Lock up any one of us for any length of time and a normal reaction to a slackening of the grip is to run!

Sometimes, paradoxically, it is the result of care and concern to establish educational progress; sitting over a pupil in what is termed a 'one-to-one' situation – almost on top of the pupil and without asking the pupil's permission. This is heightened when the pupil is in some physical difficulty and not only is an adult sitting close up to the child but also physically manipulating a part of the body – that pupil's hand, say.

In both cases what the adult may be invading is the pupil's natural space and the more the pupil is cramped the more likely it will be that tension will build up and be released in an explosion. There is a natural *personal space*, usually in humans it is approximately the distance apart of the social handshake. It is the space with which we are comfortable. Generally only those who are intimate with us (family, close friends, lovers) come closer than that distance – except, of course, in crowds, which have their own rationale and where, generally, the close proximity of another person has nothing to do with us. There is no social or emotional contact as we rub shoulders in a sports crowd or crush onto an underground train. But, in social contact, it does matter what distances people keep between themselves. Normally there are clear signs given out when someone comes too close, unless we ourselves have co-operated in closing down the space. That is the point I am making: to be comfortable, it is we who choose to allow the other person close. Pupils with difficulties, we may assume, have the same basic feelings, and yet we crowd them. Because they often do not speak or do not communicate readily in socially clear ways, it is assumed that they have no need to choose their space and staff can close space down without negotiation. It is a recipe for hostile reactions.

Of course, at times it is desirable to be close to a pupil – to hold a hand for safety, to guide a hand for stability in emphasising a track into motor memory, to prevent pupils who have been disturbed from doing damage to themselves or to others. The point to emphasise, however, is that sensitivity to personal space on the part of those around can often prevent tensions arising within pupils. Adults need permission to enter into pupil spaces and it is not affectation to ask permission even of pupils who appear unable to given voluntary consent. The timbre of voice of a courteous request is a social signal of respect that sets the tone to calm potential pupil anxiety: 'May I sit next to you?'

MARKING TIME

Along with space, staff should consider *time*. A lack of sensitivity to space – that is, to a pupil's perception of personal space – is sometimes accompanied by and exacerbated by a lack of sensitivity to a pupil's feeling for time. If the brain is processing information at a certain pace, then it is necessary to accommodate the delivery of any language, indeed of any information of any sort, to the rhythm of that mental metronome. Tension can build up very rapidly in situations where a pupil's perception of what is about to happen has not caught up with what is going on.

If that is what occurred, there is little point in addressing simply the resulting *challenging behaviour*. The professional challenge for staff should have been to plan and stage the events of a period of time (a morning, say) in such a way that each pupil had the time required to adjust to what was expected to happen. We ourselves feel harried when our perception of time is disregarded by unthinking officialdom; when, for example, we are kept waiting in the departure lounge of an airport with no explanation given of what is going on, and then suddenly we are expected to move hurriedly to another far-flung gate on a sudden announcement of an alteration.

There are various suggested programmes and organisational ways of making expected time more clear to pupils with difficulties. One way is the visual timetable that displays the day by means of photographs or symbols so that anticipated regular events can be held in the minds of pupils. But there is more to working with personal time than giving out visual timetabling. Each segment of our lives happens in time as a complex amalgam of actual clock time, in which every minute is 60 seconds in duration and so on, and emotional time, of which the length depends on our ability to adjust with involvement and interest. There is a sort of inverse ratio at work that determines that time passes speedily when we are interested and like lead when we are bored. Boredom in anyone is an adverse reactive behaviour about to happen. It is pointless telling pupils to be interested unless a lot of imagination has gone into attempting to understand how inner time works for each pupil and at what level interest can be engaged and sustained.

The most necessary strategy for working with time and engaging interest, however, does not rely on timetables but on talk. All that has been written in Chapter 4 is directly relevant not only to matters of thinking but also as a means of enabling pupils to be comfortable within their own time frame. Being comfortable goes a long way towards being without high tension. Think back a moment to our example of the departure lounge and change, not the circumstance but the way the situation was handled. Imagine that there had been friendly, apologetic, but clearly explanatory, announcements at just the right frequency during the delay telling us exactly what and why. (There is a delicate balance between irritating frequency of announcements and soothingly being kept up to date.) When the inevitable move to another gate was known, the earlier the information that allowed us as passengers to prepare for a quick dash half-way across the airport the less flustered we all would be at picking up hand luggage, finding a place to put the book we had been reading to counteract boredom, checking that we had our reading glasses in a pocket, and so on. When well handled, such a situation can be used as a paradigm of the sort of 'time language' pupils need – enough but not too much and explaining the present while creating awareness that the future will need to be organised in the mind.

TALKING IT THROUGH

Talk is of great importance as a means of enabling pupils to exercise self-control over any behaviour. Again I am thinking here of anything a pupil does as behaviour, but it is most often in moments of perceived 'bad behaviour' that a pupil is told 'Control yourself!'. This is, perhaps, an apt command but, without the understanding of what it means, how is the pupil to obey? Indeed, were the pupil capable, he or she might reply 'I *am* controlling my behaviour very well. That kick landed just where I intended'. But that, of course, is not what the teacher meant by 'control'. This takes us back to the matter of social codes and the importance of building up with pupils sets of shared definitions and explanations about the social situation of the group and the expectations inherent therein. We saw, when discussing language, (Chapter 4) that the capacity for organising thought in language (syntax) is likely to be in advance of, but not too far in advance of, the evident productive language of which the pupil is capable. This factor has to be borne in mind, also, when talking about any behaviour and seeking to define what is 'good' and what is 'bad' as a shared understanding in a relevant context. There is, however, the other side of the 'sharing' talk which is of immense benefit to the pupil. There can be no answer to the question, 'Why...?' until a pupil is able to understand and use the syntax for 'Because...!'; but, because there is no call for the structure 'because' until there has been a question 'why?', a pupil with developmental delay in language can find himself or herself in a trap with no escape: unless, that is, perceptive staff realise the difficulty and develop the necessary language (see Appendix).

I knew of a case in which a girl was reported as persistently acting in ways which irritated adults and her peer group alike. Her behaviour was described as 'attention seeking'; which was probably true, since we all are constantly seeking the attention of those around us for one reason or another – from shouting for information from someone-or-other as to where we left our car keys to ordering another bottle of wine in a restaurant. Staff said that she did not seem to understand why people found her annoying. Close analysis of her language, however, revealed that she never, spontaneously, used either a 'why?' question or the word 'because'. Many strategies to get her to be more sensitive and more socially controlled had been tried, but still it was reported 'She doesn't seem to know why she does it!'. Precisely. A way forward would be to work on her language behaviour before her social behaviour because, without access to 'because', she could not respond even to kindly staff reasoning.

There are basically three ways of structuring help and inducing the structures that are needed to answer the question 'why?' of any behaviour.

The first is by the adults in a situation explaining themselves to pupils: 'I am doing X *because...*'. Moderation in all things, of course; there will be nothing more guaranteed to turn listeners off than to have every small action self-analysed by the doer! Giving a 'because' at strategic intervals for specific situations (either important organisationally or important emotionally) introduces into the thought processes of the group at such moments the idea that there is an *implied* 'why?' in all behaviour and that things are done for a reason. Without that perception becoming part of the class social order, then all behaviour, even acceptable behaviour, will be random.

The second is by encouraging the pupils to use inner speech in all situations so that it becomes a habit. This technique was discussed on page 116 and its importance in the art of self-control of all behaviour (acceptable or challenging) can now be appreciated. When pupils can develop the link between action and motive – 'I am picking this up *because* I am going to put it in that box' – and can say this to themselves in inner speech they will have mastered the simple sequence upon which all self-understanding is based. Self-understanding, logically, must come before self-control.

We all go through a simple routine of inner speech whenever we act with intention; therefore we also go through it at times when we intend not to act. These are the two sides to self-control: voluntarily doing or not doing.

The third is by staff giving reasons for actions within the social situation. This is subtly different from the first explanatory language in that it is not so much personal (I am crying *because* I have just heard some sad news over the telephone) as a sign of group-dynamics ('We are going to do this as a group because...'). Moreover, such an introduction allows all concerned to think about the potential effects of the intended activity. There is always a danger, in any educational programme, that adults may be setting tasks for pupils without giving them a sense of being in control of their reasons for performing an action. 'Because I say so' or 'Because it's down on the programme' are scarcely adequate reasons. To give comprehensible reasons is the more, not the less, important for pupils whose reason itself may be struggling in a bid to make sense of incoming stimuli. As a general rule, if we want reasoned behaviour we have to give the reasons for it before demanding it.

FOSTERING CONTROL

For there to be an expectation of certain behaviour among pupils there must be established a climate of clear reasoning within which it can be stabilised. If this is in place, then there is the basis for fostering self-control within each member of the social group, adults and pupils alike, and the chances are that many adverse behaviours which result from boredom, bewilderment and inarticulated anger will be prevented. The more a pupil is able to assert individuality the more there will be a need for staff to think about defining what is appropriate and what is not appropriate behaviour.

Second principle
Appropriate behaviour
Appropriate behaviour should be considered against two questions:

1. Is the action socially appropriate in the relevant culture?

2. Is the action developmentally appropriate?

Is the action socially appropriate in the relevant culture?

SOCIAL CODES

Codes of behaviour, as we have seen, are not only those laid down in law. All social groups work to unwritten norms of acceptable conduct which are all the more confusing to those not intimate with the culture because they are unwritten. A person has to live for some considerable time within a particular society to be able to act wholly with confidence among these unwritten customs and usages. They are peculiar to their culture, and all those 'in the know' regard them as so self-evident as to need no explanation and thus are affronted if anyone violates them. In general, they are the oil that keeps the wheels of a society turning, and children in the culture are expected to assimilate them. Along with sorting out their vocabulary, children have to sort out 'what is done' and 'what is not done' (Dunn 1986). Young children can be seen to have minor confusions along the way and we all have memories of the bewildered embarrassment we suffered when we thought we were acting properly according to one code only to find that another code seemed to be operating. To children who find difficulty in understanding society in general, such changes in what is applied when and to whom can be abnormally confusing.

To be told off for behaviour that seems to consist purely of *manners* leaves such a pupil with bewilderment but without explanation. For example, if the action of spilling paint water on a table with other pupils' work on it is disapproved of, it has, at least, a visual component and therefore a consequence that can be seen. But the act of turning round when seated on the floor of a school hall during junior assembly when the head teacher is speaking is a matter of manner and custom in following the code of a particular school. There is a difference that has to be made between acts that are to be avoided because of antisocial consequences (say, spilling water over other pupils' work) and acts that violate a code of manners. We have already seen how manners should be approached ('We don't do that here') in contrast to how antisocial behaviour *per se* should be approached ('That is not a good thing to do *because...*').

CODE AND CULTURE

A more sensitive concern, however, in judging whether behaviour of a pupil with severe difficulties is appropriate or not, is the need to ask whether the school rule that makes that behaviour appropriate or inappropriate comes from a particular social group to which the pupil may not have had ready access. Never is this more so than when a cross-cultural element is involved. For example, the rules of polite table manners differ in cultures which use fingers as the tools of eating and those which use knives and forks. A pupil attempting to put fingers into food in a school dining hall may be acting according to strict rules of eating from one culture, only to be confused by disapprobation and punishment in another. Analysis of such a behaviour might well reveal that what was termed 'inappropriate' and called 'messy eating' was not the finger eating itself (the behaviour) but an enforced selection from inappropriately prepared food. A meal designed for knife and fork often lacks the necessary breads and rice that facilitate use of fingers, hence eating with the fingers becomes messy and ineffective, and subject to the rule of a different cultural background – 'Good children don't put their fingers in their food'. Yet at home that is precisely what good children are expected to do, provided they obey the code of which hand is used for what purpose and in what manner.

What has been written so far is not to argue against teaching rules across cultural diversity but it is to emphasise that such rules of conduct are not *absolutes* and the behaviour of a pupil with severe difficulties should be assessed both in a cultural context and also with a recognition of the arbitrariness of many of the things required to be done by and in any particular society.

Is the action developmentally appropriate?

IS AGE A SURE GUIDE TO BEHAVIOUR?

There is much confusion about the concept of *age-appropriate* behaviour. The confusion lies behind such disapproving remarks as 'Be your age' and implies that someone somewhere can disclose a set of norms as to what is applicable to various ages. Nor is it confined to developmental stages. It may equally be heard in remarks addressed to a boy of ten who is seen crying or to a pensioner of 90 going out night-clubbing every night. In both cases we have to ask why should the person concerned not be doing that particular action at that particular age? Certainly there are developmental norms which chart the expected abilities of infants and young children, for example Sheridan (1975), at various ages and in this sense we can see whether a child measures up within the expected age range, but it is a description of *range*, not an exact series of measurements. With group expectations for social behaviour, however, comes the idea of what is expected with increasing age. Again this is culturally based and customs vary from culture to culture.

Another concept that often arises is that of 'mental age'. This seems to involve a strange idea that the mind has an age norm independent of the brain age. It is used, for example, as a shorthand by judges in legal cases where there has been brain damage and a claim is being pursued. It is used as an emotional oversimplification in the media and it is used with a more technical association by psychologists as a consequence of pursuing IQ calculations against standardised 'age norms'.

Age, however, is a complex concept. At its simplest it is the time from the point of birth to the present moment, which is generally termed 'chronological age'. And that is really all that it can be. Everything else is a fabrication – a comparison with a purely theoretical expectation about what anyone *ought* to do at any given point in time according to the view of the speaker. Strictly speaking, that point could be any defined moment which the speaker had chosen – say, 3.30 p.m. on 30 September. One could then say, 'This child is behaving as if he had a mental age of 3.20 p.m. on 24 September.' Clearly, saying that would lead to ridicule. But why is it any less ridiculous to say 'He has a mental age three years behind his chronological age', except that the period is longer and therefore appears to carry more seriousness and weight? As a statement, however, it is equally meaningless. The danger is that it may lead people to treat that individual person, often an adult, as if responses to him or to her were appropriately based upon what people would say to or do with a child of a chronological age equivalent to the postulated 'mental age'.

In analysing behaviour we have to ask whether what we are doing is enabling the child or adult to develop, to grow up, even allowing their inherent difficulties; or whether, on the contrary, we are allowing the idea of age to trap the child or adult in the very arbitrary idea of their being frozen and never capable of making any further development of any sort.

DEVELOPMENT IN SOME WAY GOES ON

Even if it is allowed that the 'mind' has an existence independent of 'the brain' (Bartsch and Wellman 1995), the idea of a mental age divorced from consideration of what is happening to the body as a whole is surely untenable. There will be parts of the brain that will gain a maturity willy-nilly, and they in turn will affect the operations of a 'mind', however independently that is defined.

To take only one example. There will be, with growth, sexual development that is purely biological. The sex urge is a factor of puberty and biochemistry – not of mind. So even if it is to be argued that 'mind' in humans controls that particular urge in socially profitable ways – or not, as the case may be – it is clear that an 18 year old with a so-called 'mental age' of, say, three years is not experiencing three-year-old sexual drives because the drives of a three year old are not stemming from the mature sexual brain biochemistry of an 18 year old.

It is more profitable to put the matter of age appropriateness differently. When considering behaviour we have to seek a balance of interpretation between the developmental stage at which any action (considered purely as a behaviour) would be accepted as appropriate and the chronological age of the pupil. This allows us to look for the *significance* of the behaviour. A pupil of 14 may be sucking her thumb. Thumb sucking is not generally regarded as socially appropriate in a girl of 14 years. It is associated with a developmental stage of two to three years old. What that assessment tells us is that there is a developmental lag within the pupil – remember, we are attempting to work *from the inside* in all our understanding of behaviour – that may or may not need to be addressed. The behaviour may not be age appropriate as far as her chronological age is concerned but may well be significant as far as her emotional progress is concerned. At one and the same time as sucking her thumb she may well be making apparently gauche attempts to come into contact with teenage boys. Again this behaviour, although in one sense age appropriate (that is, arising from pubertal drives), may lead to other behaviours that are thought to be against the social code – lifting her dress, for example. When analysed in total, however, the tensions within the behaviour become the more apparent and the girl might be seen, from the inside, as attempting to come to terms with the hormonal drives of puberty, with some of the experiences of 14 years, and yet be doing this within many of the restrictions of the emotional development (for whatever reason) normally arising from the experience of a three year old. It would be no wonder, given this analysis, that her behaviour might confuse her and confuse others. But it would do her no good at all to regard her as, and treat her as, a three year old.

The first question, 'Is the action (and the specific action alone) age-appropriate?' is therefore to be asked as a means of establishing where there may be significant gaps in development, to the bewilderment of the pupil: not as a source of condemnation of the pupil for 'not growing up'. The second question, then, is: 'At what developmental stage is the action appropriate?' The comparison between the two answers gives an analytical means of considering how to approach such a behaviour in the interests of the pupil in question and, by such a comparison, may also suggest stages by which both to target progressive steps and to assess development.

Implications for teaching

Appropriateness

SOCIALLY APPROPRIATE BEHAVIOUR

Staff are always faced with holding a difficult balance between the actual needs of individual pupils and the well-being of the whole. This is a fact of classroom management not peculiar to the education of pupils with severe difficulties. There is always a judgement to be made as to whether behaviour, of whatever description, is 'appropriate' or not.

Cultural determinants can be broadly considered. Some rules concern safety and these are to be included in *culture*. All social order has to have within it a concern for safety. When, however, it comes to particular social cultures becoming adjacent, as in communities with transient populations, then care has to be taken not to impose without reason one behaviour upon another. It is right to develop a behaviour in any pupil in order that that pupil may move the more comfortably within another desirable culture. It is important, however, to study the necessity or otherwise of the new cultural norm, not simply to impose it. An example often used in this respect is the culturally determined norm in certain children of dropping the eyes when speaking to an elder, as a note of respect and acknowledgement of the authority of the adult. In many classrooms, however, and certainly with pupils in difficulties, the adults demand 'Look at me when I'm talking to you'. There may be times when, in the culture of the particular classroom, eye contact is desirable, but it is important to consider what social rules might govern such a condition and to make them explicit.

It is in age appropriateness that the greatest difficulty may arise for the teacher. Clearly all societies work with certain unspoken expectations of behaviours that mature with increased age in a person. In a classroom in which there are pupils who have severe difficulties there will inevitably arise a tension between what is developmentally necessary for a particular pupil and what would be appropriate given that pupil's chronological age within the social culture of a peer group. To deny the necessary experience to any pupil at each stage in development is to hamper important education; however, to allow behaviour that clashes with the social and cultural expectations placed upon the individual may well be to confuse and to upset. Such behaviours, in the past and often, have been the ones that 'justified' shutting such pupils away from the gaze of the populace in general (Hurt 1988). How is the dilemma to be resolved in the interests of the pupil?

As we have seen, a teacher wishing to answer this question has to go back to an analysis of the behaviour itself, not its effect, and ask the further question, 'What is the function of that behaviour for the pupil at this stage of experience and development?'. There follows a second important question, 'Is there an age-appropriate behaviour that would serve the same experiential and developmental function?'. If the answer to the latter question is 'Yes', then the decision is one of method: how to change the one behaviour into the other, giving the pupil reasons for the adult's actions along the way. The initial observation necessary before determining the import of many behaviours has been gone into in Chapter 3. Here we can deal more appropriately with the technique for moving behaviours towards more age-appropriate ends.

Let us take two exemplar behavioural needs, referring back to the discussion in the first part of this chapter. *Thumb sucking* is a stage in the transition from the focus on oral gratification and comfort to a stage of social self-awareness in most ordinary infant development. If it perpetuates, however, it may well signal a hiatus in the social self-awareness of a pupil in difficulty and an inability to move out of the self-comforting zone into a confident ability to gain that comfort from social interactions. Therefore the age-appropriate progression at which to aim is increased ability and confidence in interchanges with staff and other pupils. Paying undue attention to the act of thumb sucking without working towards the developmental behaviour that normally absorbs it will not generally stop the impulse. What must be developed in its place must be some habit that gives the pupil a more mature ability to find appropriate social comfort. Preventative methods (such as tying down hands, which was once a not uncommon practice in 'mental care') are largely conveying the wrong message: that it is emotionally wrong to need comfort! The move away from this particular behaviour, therefore, involves positive attention to interpersonal development and the skills of dialogue in the context of emotional needs.

When it comes to *sexual* behaviours, moving the ability to experience pleasure away from an infant level of perception into a more mature adult awareness is often a source of difficulty for staff. One of the continual problems is that physical development, under the control of biochemical energy, often creates impulses in a pupil for which the mind is out of sync. Are apparent sexual behaviours, therefore, to be assessed against their apparent physical purpose or against their emotional content?

SEXUAL MATTERS

Sexual matters are not simply a staff problem. Sexual instinct and sexually driven subconscious impulses at the biological level can cause painful confusions in pupils if their self-awareness and social awareness levels are not attuned to cope. The apparent hormonal upsets and agonies that are normally observed in adolescence will be no less present in pupils in difficulties of learning even when their capacity to express them in more recognisable adolescent fashion, either in physical defiance of convention or in melancholy bouts of passion, may not be readily within their repertoires. Confused behaviour is then to be expected. Such behaviour is not necessarily aggressive. It is often fear in the observer rather than reality that makes an inevitable link between male sexuality and aggression in those with learning difficulties. The pattern as a whole is as diverse as that of any adolescent population in this regard. What will certainly be observed, if staff are on the look-out for such behaviours, is increased social clumsiness towards members of the opposite sex, curiosity, tension, periods of depressive sadness and confusion. What will be happening is an internal anxiety caused by physical changes – erections, menstruation, facial hair, breast development – all the normal things, but occurring in an adolescent whose safe concept of *self* may not have yet been helped in its maturity to a point where there is sufficient self-understanding.

There are some developing emotional behaviour patterns that can be observed in infants, wherein there is an apparent sexual element but which largely reflect the exploration of 'self'. The most obvious example is *masturbation*. Feelings of pleasure through the erogenous zones, the genitals or the pudenda, is a lifelong condition; whether the stimulation is 'age appropriate' depends on many things and demands that the behaviour is viewed against many possible criteria. Again, however, as in the matter of thumb sucking, one of the main criteria is the level of language that a pupil can use in self-awareness.

Masturbation at the level of an infant's dawning bodily self-awareness is, properly, socially unacceptable in a pupil above the age of five years or so. It certainly will cause anxiety in a classroom if the pupil is beyond puberty. Yet to seek to suppress the one aspect, the developmental need, in consideration of a pupil's inability to cope with the other, the sexual social restraint, in an age appropriate way may not be to meet the educational needs of that pupil.

The problem, of course, is that physical development introduces more complexities than mere self-exploration. Staff can sometimes be observed addressing what they consider the appropriate emotional and developmental needs in a manner that would be acceptable were the pupils at the chronological age of their assumed emotional development but which, given their real age, is making life difficult for them. Demonstrations of physical affection may be a case in point. Children need contact as part of their development and we all need cuddles from time to time. Pupils with difficulties would not be well served by adults who wished them nothing but good yet failed to take account of the confusions that were arising, if they based the contacts they had with pupils on the premise of their 'mental age' and failed to realise that the 'biological age' of the pupil was triggering potentially bewildering inner conflict. For a nubile teacher to give a friendly cuddle to a pupil, as one would to a child of two years old or so, is not an act towards a two-year-old developmental level when the recipient has had thirteen years of biological growth. Such acts are inappropriate, not because of the physical contact but because of the thoughtlessness about the instinctive confusions that may arise and which the pupil has not the developed thought process to cope with. Similarly, it is inappropriate, at least in cultures where there is not a lot of embracing and kissing in general social situations, for the 13 year old to express social greeting by running up to anyone and kissing her or him full in the mouth. It may well be different, and more productive of a pupil's general social understanding and physical need for contact, in cultures where greeting between good friends involves hugging and kissing on both cheeks. It is then less difficult to steer the behaviour of seeking contact both bodily and osculatory into socially acceptable, age-appropriate channels – although even in this case it is unusual for pupils to rush up to teachers in this way! So the requirement, in attempting to balance (chronological) age-appropriate socially acceptable behaviour and the pupil's need for developmentally appropriate contact, is to look for a neutral set of behaviours that can be appropriate for both parties at all levels of analysis. Again there is importance in nurturing the development of language; explaining to the pupil a positive way to interact physically with different people. Be careful not to say that kissing is wrong; it is the social contextual appropriateness, not the act itself, that is in question. Not kissing mummy because of a taught inhibition to the act at school would be inappropriate and one must not prevent the behaviour itself when it is part of normal sexual maturity. For such behaviours, at the crossroads of puberty, the context is all.

Third principle

Responsibility must be conscious of the origins

PRIME QUESTION. WAS THERE AN INTENTION TO PERPETRATE?

I now turn to the questions of *blame or praise*. It is a general assumption in all social situations that everyone knows what he or she is doing and is therefore responsible for his or her actions. Antisocial acts, therefore, attract blame and courageous acts attract adulation and approbation. We are not used to asking the question, 'Did the people concerned know what they were doing when they did it?'. I have already touched upon punishment linked to contravention of a code where the breach in the code is the reason for taking action, not the assumed inner state of the offender. Now, however, we are coming from the position of attempting to understand the behaviour via the 'inside out' route: asking, 'What is really going on in the mind of the pupil?'.

Intention is an act of the will considered in the conscious mind. If I *intend* to do you harm, then I have to know something about you, even if only that you are in some way, at that moment, someone whom I do not like, and I have to realise that what I do will, in fact, in some way cause you to be discomforted. There is an element of planning present, even if sudden and brief. In other words, I must, at the time of the action, understand cause and effect and have the capacity to use inner language to plan. This would hold good for all physical acts intended to cause injury or pain.

Several factors among pupils with severe difficulties may prevent these preconditions operating.

The first difficulty may arise from the underdevelopment of *discourse*. As we saw in Chapter 5, such a linguistic restriction simply does not allow the experimentation that enables us to sound out the minds of others. The mechanisms for teasing the information out of another person may simply not be in place (Rondal and Edwards 1997).

The second difficulty is that the action in focus may not follow intention. Actions of this type should strictly be described as *re*-actions in the pupil. Whenever there is severe functional impairment of the brain that must remain a possibility. This is not simply confined to one of the accepted types of epilepsy (O'Donohoe 1985), although some forms of focal epilepsy do result in pupils taking actions of which they are momentarily unconscious and therefore have no intention of performing. The effect of less definable brain interference, however, is virtually the same because it results in what is not a voluntary action on the pupil's part. An example would be a sudden jerk of an arm that hits another pupil or knocks over a beaker of water but which does not appear in the records as an expected part of an already diagnosed medical condition. Unless such episodes are observed by an experienced staff member as they occur, then there is the real danger that pupils will be treated as *blameworthy* for actions that are the result of such an 'episode' and of which only the results are seen. Concentrating on the result of an act of which the pupil has no conscious knowledge is potentially bewildering, and if the pupil is aware (however imperfectly) of resulting *blame*, very distressing. One of the reasons for an increase in adverse behaviour may be that the pupil simply has no awareness of cause and effect in the context. This momentary disconnection may happen more frequently among pupils with severe difficulties than people realise. Even a second of unawareness can disconnect the realisation of the link between cause and effect. The instant is not often observed unless staff are acting as detectives.

A case study might go some way to illustrate what I mean.

YY was a physically large 15-year-old girl in a school for pupils with severe difficulties. She had some speech but this was mainly confined to single word utterances or echoic phrases of which 'bad girl' was one. Staff had become disturbed by her apparently random outbursts of aggressive behaviour and nonconformity with the group. She tended to be clumsy and often knocked things over on a work table. When in a group she sometimes became belligerent when addressed and then seemed to act contrary to any instruction she had just been given. When she had done something to disrupt the lesson she would often stand addressing no one in particular and say, 'Bad girl, bad girl'. The fact that she used these words in these circumstances was taken to be an indication that she was *deliberately* setting out to challenge staff and was becoming uncontrollable.

In order to attempt to determine what was really going on with this pupil *from the inside* the educational psychologist and an SEN adviser requested a videotape of a complete day, and this was duly provided by the school.

Careful analysis of the videotape, often necessitating frame-by-frame study of details, revealed that the girl appeared to be having momentary 'blank' episodes, the evidence for which was the sudden fixation of her gaze combined with autonomic movements (jerks of the body) lasting at most four seconds but occurring a number of times in any one hour. In one particular incident, the girl was using poster paints with brushes dipped in water – an activity that she clearly enjoyed and was reportedly good at – and, in reaching her brush towards the water, entered one of these brief spells, lasting two seconds. Her hand jerked forward, knocked over the water container, froze for an instant and then the phase passed. The reaction of staff was predictable, given that as yet they had not observed for intermittent discontinuity. She was upbraided. She reacted to the clear blame from those around her with the stock phrase 'Bad girl' and this was taken by staff at the time to indicate that she knew very well what had happened and that her knocking over of the water had been a deliberate act resulting in the ruination of her work and that of another pupil.

In terms of the analysis of her behaviour, however, this interpretation presented a grave problem. At the moment of impact, which was played frame by frame in analysis in order to be as certain as possible about what was to be seen, she clearly did not have any focus upon what her hand was doing. When her look refocused it was to see water all over the table which, immediately before her blank moment, was in a jar standing before her.

The use of 'Bad girl' throughout the day also had a pattern. It followed such apparent episodes and was triggered by the overt blame she was being subjected to. From her general demeanour it appeared more that she was reacting with appeasement behaviour, saying in effect, 'I don't know why you're angry but I must be what you call "bad girl"', than that she was rejoicing in her ability to make fools out of staff and the rest of her group. It was a conditioned response, most probably learned from the many times when it had been said to her following a blank episode. She seemed to be following a set conditioned-response pattern: when there is discontinuity, say 'Bad girl'.

Once staff, on the evidence of the video, were willing to rethink what was happening, they were able to reinterpret much of their irritation with her. They could experiment with the idea that she failed to carry out instructions or did the wrong thing because she had missed a crucial part of the sequence of instructions; but not through *deliberate* in-attention. Indeed, there had been inconsistency in their notion that she was deliberately trying to be a bad girl. She clearly did not plan most of her day and staff were used to guiding her at every trick and turn. At one and the same time, but without it being realised, she was treated as helpless and cunning. One or other incompatible condition had to be incorrect.

The belligerence that occurred – her stubborn refusal at times to move at all – could be explained as a panic reaction to not knowing what was going on – to having lost the thread. When a general interactional strategy was devised based on these insights, giving her time to adjust and providing repeat instructions to allow her to pick up the whole of a sequence even if there was a momentary discontinuity during the giving of them, she began to relax. The staff did, as well. Offering reassurance rather than blame after some physical clumsiness also lessened the 'bad girl' reaction.

It should be remembered that the judgemental values placed upon 'good' and 'bad' by adults are difficult for pupils with severe difficulties to comprehend. For any child it is an advanced linguistic development to be able to distil the meaning of either word out of the social usages in everyday speech. We saw above how complex codes can be. The accom-panying vocabulary – of what is 'good' and what is 'bad' – makes the task of understanding almost impossible for any pupil whose linguistic progress has been limited and whose social sense is rudimentary. For a pupil with a limited *theory of mind* (see Chapter 5) the reason in the mind of the adult for praising or blaming is obscured. It is rare for a pupil to be given a contextual explanation of the mind of the adult when being called 'Bad girl'. It would have to go something like this:

> I am using the term 'bad girl' for what has just happened because I think in my mind that you calculated that it would annoy me greatly and make me show that I was at the end of my tether if you knocked over that jar of water. I have an adverse emotional reaction to being treated like this. Moreover the water has ruined not only your own work, which you seemed yesterday to be proud of (but now to have deliberately ruined), but also that of your friend. What the reason is for your wishing to upset her, I can't imagine. What you calculated in your

mind and its effects upon my mind, in combination, are sufficient reason for me to use the term 'bad' which refers to the general disturbance you have occasioned in the smooth social atmosphere and easy management of this class and the headache I have which has been made worse by what you have just done.

And yet something of that order of understanding is assumed in the pupil when the term is used by an adult in reaction to that pupil. Perhaps, if we had to give contextual explanations every time we used the word 'bad', we would think more about what we meant, how complex the references were and what each pupil might understand by it. Little children, in developing their language, can be heard to ask (sometimes interminably) for case instances upon which to generate a working definition: 'Mummy, am I being "good"? Daddy, was I "good" when I did X?' In any classroom day, with pupils with severe difficulties, it is worth examining whether they are given encouragement to seek clarification in this way. It is not enough, however, merely to tell them, without their asking, that they are 'being good' in phrases such as 'good sitting', 'good writing'. There is a need to help them to understand what is meant by *intention* to be good.

The nature of an intention to do X involves the capacity for *reasoning*; for being able to work out a plan and form it into a strategic action. This capacity is observable early in infant development but, significantly, may be apparently missing in children with severe difficulties, as observations of their play has suggested (Astington 1994). Here, however, a caution is in order. While, in developmental terms, the capacity for such planning may be impaired, it needs careful observation to determine that it is completely missing. Children's play is often observed solely with the mind of an adult which means that the adult is not seeing what is happening 'from the child's point of view'. The adult has to ask 'Why is the pupil playing in that way?' to determine if actions are really purposeless and random or whether they contain an element of planning.

If a child is not exhibiting an adequate capacity to reason in his or her general classroom activities and is not showing simple cause and effect (as far as can be deduced) in play, then it will be unsafe to ascribe complex intention to any item of behaviour. Of course, a simple motor act, such an act as picking up a knife, will be with simple intention (I see a knife, I extend my hand and I lift the knife with that hand) but further than that – to ascribe to the pupil a plan as to what *effect* an act with the knife might have – requires the ability to employ reason.

The application of the corollary to this principle provides a useful safeguard against a too ready use of *blame*. The justification for blaming a pupil for an action rests upon a judgement as to how far the pupil has both the inner-language and the sense of other minds to be able to form an intention. If there is a shadow of a doubt as to the presence of both these factors, then look for an explanation that accords in all particulars with the pupil's demonstrable understanding. Ascribing blame without being able to demonstrate the capacity to intend will lead to confusion in the pupil and is likely to increase rather than limit the behaviours in question.

Implications for teaching

Conscious of and in control of?

The most upsetting behaviours challenge us by being in the grey area: does the pupil understand what he or she is doing or not? While learning behaviours where it is important for the pupil to have an intention in a task have been dealt with in Chapter 5, I want now to turn attention to the many instances of adverse behaviours which staff find extreme. These are actions which result in the potential damage to the pupil and in the distress caused to bystanders, who may often be other young persons with no direct, immediate involvement in the circumstances of the incident. Was the action intended or not?

Intention does not reside in the behaviour itself but at a stage before that behaviour takes place. Such behaviour must be analysed, therefore, from a clear baseline of the pupil's cognitive and linguistic capability. If, for example, the pupil is not considered yet capable of planning a cognitive strategy in a classroom activity – that action A will be followed by action B – then it is inconsistent on the part of an adult to argue that the pupil *planned* a behaviour such that action X would cause reaction Y. Similarly, if the overt language level of a pupil (that is, what the pupil can clearly communicate by whatever means) and if the assumptions that can be made about carefully observed inner speech do not both indicate that the pupil is using some simple self-analysis ('I think therefore I can show intention') then once more it is dangerous to assume that an action was planned, carried through and ultimately contemplated with enjoyment or satisfaction because it was deliberately perverse or against an accepted code of conduct.

At this point it has to be borne in mind, however, that all children go through a developmental stage when their own place in the world is the arena for their experimentation precisely because their inner language is confused. Children, both in the 'terrible twos' and in adolescence, go through periods of testing out boundaries. With such antecedents, confusing behaviours are not so much a direct attack upon the adults around as they are a (somewhat uncomfortable) experiment within the child/adolescent. That the adult shall be challenged is not the intention of the instigator of the behaviour, even if it is the net result. The personality being challenged is that of the child or young person, personally and internally. The behaviour itself, in such an instance, is communicating a call for clarification – of boundaries, emotions, relationships and suchlike complexities – and should be reacted to as such.

There are times, however, when an eruption of adverse behaviour in a pupil does not allow staff time for calm contemplation of its origins, when safety and containment are the immediate concern.

It is in the handling (literally) of pupils out of their own control that we enter a field riddled with potential controversy. There are reasons why some physical interference may have to happen in a fraught situation if the safety of a pupil and those around is to be preserved. What guidance should staff follow to work through such episodes of such behaviour?

GUIDANCE NOTES

It is suggested that staff should work out an agreed Code of Practice for addressing such situations so that there will be consistency in the action taken, independent of who is faced with the behaviour. Prethought-out approaches and confidence that any action taken will be within the consensus of colleagues and parents is a means of preparing staff to take appropriate action without the need to think of anything in a situation except the immediate needs of the pupil. It also establishes for pupils a confident situation. From the point of view of the pupil in a panic state, a lack of a confident approach by an adult only exacerbates the distress that panic always induces. Panic arises in the deep-seated areas of the brain where indeed other instincts, such as smell of fear and visual signals from the features of adults around that our linguistic sense usually tends to supplant, are alerted.

To this end – working out a classroom code of practice – careful attention should be paid to the positive and helpful use of language-to-a-purpose in situations of adverse behaviour.

If a pupil, usually in control of what he or she is doing, appears about to 'lose it', then it may be possible to arrest the tension before it takes the pupil over, as it were. Here, the member of staff begins by relying on voice alone. Things rapidly slide out of control if physical contact is prematurely forced upon the pupil. We know, from our own experiences, that if we are in a heightened state of tension, being touched or, worse, grabbed will push us over the edge and we are likely to shrug off the contact forcefully. The voice, however, is both a safer and a more effective first weapon. At any point before a pupil slips over into a rage state it may be possible, by a quiet but sharp word to gain sufficient of his or her attention, to enable some reasoning to remain in the situation.

Basic use of language is with a very soft and encouraging voice. It may, at first, seem paradoxical for me to recommend a staff member to encourage a pupil who is in a heightened state but what is to be encouraged is the knowledge that control *will* return. 'OK, OK. It's feeling rough at the moment but you will get the calm back. You will!' Part of the horror of a panic state, from the inside, is that it has taken away the expectation that calm and mental peace will ever return. One of the factors to ensure confidence in a member of staff in handling the situation is also that control, from the inside of the pupil, *will* return. The two aspects of the situation are served by the same tone of language. Correction will only take if the pupil is in a calm enough state to understand it and accept it.

In a panic state, what he or she is doing will not be clear in the pupil's mind. Even if the pupil is vaguely aware of what he or she is doing, then it is likely that there is also an awareness of not being able to stop it. Rather like the brain of an addict, the mechanisms of control, even if vaguely desired, are not powerful enough to prevent the behaviour taking over. Something more than merely saying 'Stop it!' is required. Where behaviour does resemble an addiction, in this sense, is that it appears the pupil at least has some realisation of what is happening – and does not know how to stop it. He or she is aware that the action is happening but it is separated from voluntary control. Under these circumstances, it is sometimes useful to pupil and teacher for an adult to model to the pupil what is going on. Take the instance of hand self-biting. If the adult mimes biting her or his own hand, the pupil will take control of the situation by pulling the adult's hand away from the bite. The key to the strategy is that by setting the action in front of the pupil, the adult allows the pupil to practise the mental exercise of *taking control*. The pupil must go through the physical act (taking the hand away) and the thought pattern of control itself before being able to practise *self-control*.

With behaviours over which the pupil has minimal control, it is in no one's interest to attempt to start in the middle, demanding internal control before the pupil is aware of what is entailed in such control – taking the hand away from the mouth, for example. That is, quite simply, starting from the wrong end! Until pupils have an understanding of what it means to be in a *positive state*, such as controlled, calm, relaxed, there is no point in telling them to be in such a state. It can only confuse matters. Similarly, if they have motor impulses to acts such as self-biting, then they have to be able to mobilise counter-actions by way of a conscious motor programme. Taking the mental and physical step of pulling the adult's hand away is setting up a necessary *counter-action* to self-biting and at the same time reinforcing the action of prevention in the conscious intention of the pupil.

Once more (as we saw in Chapter 5) it is a matter of starting with the answer first if learning is to take place.

The code, as agreed, should recommend using whatever chance presents itself, when the pupil is unflustered, to do two things. First, to reinforce by words of explanation (in the mode discussed in Chapter 2) the inner feeling of a desired state (of control, etc.) so that the pupil builds up an awareness of the feelings experienced in the state indicated by 'Control yourself!'. Second, to think about the matter as a *trigger.* The disturbing factor to adults around such incidents of challenging behaviour is precisely the fact that the action arrives unexpectedly. In seeking to instil 'the answer first', it is also possible to work towards instilling positive triggers to maintain a desired inner state. This is not as strange as it may sound. It is only to incorporate into a more formal code the developmental control patterns that good parenting engenders into the family circle, as when the infant looks to the mother when aware of an impulse to commit some act or other – say picking a flower from the garden next door – in order to check whether it is an OK thing to do. If there is a slight shake of the head or a warning raising of the eyebrow, then the trigger signal, 'watch it', has been given and the action is inhibited. If the child receives the signal and goes ahead with the action anyway, then we are facing a different sort of action which will be the subject of discussions under 'Fourth principle'.

Fourth principle
Intention must be consistent with the level of thinking
THE REVERSE HOLDS GOOD

If a pupil, all things having been considered, appears to have perpe-trated a behaviour requiring sophisticated thought, then that pupil should be presented with work that exercises the mind to that level. The evidence of such an action is evidence of a capacity for cognitive processes that require to be stimulated. The arguments I have put forward throughout this book lead to a focus on the development of intentionality in each pupil. The best guide to the use that pupils are making of any language is to observe carefully how they can marshal their capacity to think. Analysis of this evidence gives the clue to their inner speech (see Chapters 4 and 5). It is the process that is going on in a pupil's mind that will determine both what he or she can intend and how far she or he can interpret what is happening.

It is here that adults need to exercise their own *theory of mind*, seeking in their imaginations to understand what the circumstances of a behaviour look like from the inside out. The importance of imagination as a teaching tool was discussed in Chapter 1. The importance of observation was discussed in Chapter 3. Staff need to use imagination based on observation to deduce whether a pupil is showing intentionality.

Basically, the test of intentionality is whether the pupil can offer an explanation (any explanation) of why the behaviour is happening. We discussed how, in order to do this, the pupil must have the linguistic development to operate a 'because' construction in answer to a 'why?' question, as well as some concept of the social structure that defines how behaviour is regarded. It is pointless demanding explanation from pupils whose language level is not so sophisticated or of those who are without an appreciation of how actions may be viewed by the enquirer.

Panic is the classic behaviour from instinct rather than intentionality. People in panic do not behave rationally. It is, perhaps, the ultimate example of acting purely on unmodified body-brain chemistry. The feeling, from the inside, is unpleasant, indeed terrifying, but the victim literally does not know why. It is often assumed that panic is the result of terror; but it is more likely that the feelings we identify as 'real terror' are part and parcel of the panic itself. The well-documented apparent liking that children have for 'being frightened' – for example, by fairy stories – is most likely to be a useful social way to control possible panic in real situations by experiencing a play version of it in the safety of the here and now. Some behaviour in some pupils with severe difficulties shows all the outward appearances of being driven by the same biochemistry that overtakes rational thought in all people when thrust into panic situations. There is a great difference between behaviour that is deliberately 'naughty' (that is, has been deliberated over in the mind) and behaviour that has, for the moment, taken over the pupil, resulting in unintentional feelings which leads him or her into a state bordering on panic.

The corollary also offers the opposite, but equally important, point of view. If, after careful observation, a teacher becomes convinced that a pupil is indeed 'playing her up' and there is evidence of that pupil's intentionality, then, however unpleasant the item of behaviour in question, there is positive evidence of inner reasoning and the potential needs to be exploited. There is something illogical in pupils who are reportedly capable of planning elaborate actions to reduce staff to tears being sat in front of repetitive and largely predigested tasks that are not exploiting that same capacity to reason.

Implications for teaching

Intention and thinking

What if the pupil shows a degree of inner language and cognitive capacity and yet still does unacceptable things? What if the teacher is convinced that there is an element of deliberate and wilful challenge?

All things depend on the developmental levels of inner language, the pupil's cognitive ability and the context in which the behaviours are being displayed. If there are many behaviours that are not even being considered because they are not challenging and these are set in the balance against the behaviours that staff find irritating, then a sense of proportion is established. Setting down a sense of proportion is a key role for the detective. The result will allow staff to move away from the temptation to concentrate on a single item in a whole behaviour pattern and to discuss the purpose of the challenging item of behaviour in its whole context.

Taking all behavioural patterns into consideration, the most likely indicators that a pupil is emerging late through natural developmental stages towards a level of self-reliant maturity – irritating though the process may be – is provided by behaviour that is generally lumped under the heading of 'testing boundaries'. Boundary testing is a natural way for a child to establish both an identity and a dependency: testing out both how far the social circle will allow independence and thereby establishing the sense of individuality itself. It is essentially a far more complex business than that a child is simply 'trying to get away with it'. In a sense the child is trying *not* to get away with it; that is, to learn that he or she has come to the edge of the boundary of what is individual and is reaching into the realm of the rules of the social group. This is a complex area allied to the first *principal principle* – realisation of self-identity – that was discussed in Chapter 1 and which was developed via the third *principal principle* – active experiment. It is an area fraught with mistakes on any child's part. It is also an area where the role of the teacher is to make explicit precisely where the boundaries are, not as punishment, because it is natural for the pupil to explore them, but as an *educational* experience that impresses upon the pupil his or her role in the context in which the action is taking place; because we do not do that in acceptable social circles, we do not do that in the supermarket, or we do not do that because it is harmful to our own selves or others.

How that is done effectively will depend on the capacity of the pupil to reason in language. Again, the assumed inner-speech capacity is the key to the effectiveness of educational approaches. If the pupil is apparently testing out boundaries but has not yet reached a stage in language when conditional syntax is part of the reasoning process – 'If you were to do that then you would…' – then it is likely that a direct prohibition at the point of action will be necessary. If, for example, the pupil is testing out crossing a boundary, say a doorway, then it may be necessary to work in the doorway in order to establish by often quite forceful emphatic body language (perhaps finger raising and tight mouth muscles) and simple negatives ('No! No!') that that doorway is a boundary and there is nothing more to be said. The mistake often made is that it is the adult, as well as the child, who crosses the boundary – the adult chasing the child – and the resulting mixed messages for the pupil only confuse the very boundary that is being tested. At best it then turns into a game of chase; at worst it negates the presumed original intention on the part of the pupil – to test a physical boundary. When teachers complain that pupils are deliberately testing them out it is as well to pause and consider. Are the staff standing at some boundary in the pupil's mind?

No one will suggest that pupils are allowed simply to run across boundaries with no one caring! This is not the point being made here; and, indeed, if the pupil is 'a runner', simply driven by an unconsidered impulse to run and run, that behaviour should be addressed in terms of the previous *principle*. But when the pupil is genuinely, if confusedly, testing a boundary then, however fleetingly, the pupil will give a backward glance to see if the adult is following. Where the adult is standing, at the point of the glance back, is establishing the boundary. It is not easy to stand stock still at the boundary and indicate to the pupil that she or he has to return to the crossing point of his or her own will; but, if a boundary is to be established, then it is necessary. This aspect of positive behaviour strategies should also form part of a code, as agreed, outlined in the previous section. When there is a safety boundary, such as shut gates and a fence to an area, then it is safe to allow the pupil the room to find what is in effect a boundary of comfort, defined as the point where sudden anxiety at having tested out that boundary cuts in to the consciousness and where the pupil can and will move back towards the awaiting adult. Where there is less immediate boundary, through the corridors of a school, for example, then it should be part of the accepted code of a school that other members of staff will provide the safety but, having stopped the pupil and turned him or her back, will allow the pupil to return to the awaiting adult as an act of will, not of constraint. If constraint is used (and it may have to be) then it has to be realised that *self*-control of boundaries will not be taught and the pupil will miss out on necessary developmental stages.

If the pupil has reached a level of linguistic development which allows conditional syntax, then it is possible to move into more sophisticated ways of influencing self-control: giving reasons for things and helping pupils to find reasons for what they have done. The more complex the reasons that teachers project onto pupils for behaviours that the pupils commit, the more it ought to imply that the pupils have the language of basic reasoning. If a teacher is tempted to say of a pupil: 'He does that because he knows...' then it must mean, if it is a true judgement, that the pupil has the capacity for inner reasoning.

It is at this point that the importance of the corollary to this principle comes into play. If there is such a degree of inner reasoning that increasingly complex *motives* can be attributed to pupils, then there is no excuse for failing to challenge this capacity in lessons (Sugden 1989). Often it appears that pupils thought capable of complex motivation in planning their adverse behaviour are not challenged sufficiently by complex reasoning tasks in the work set. With the increasing emphasis in education today on progressive outcomes and the raising of standards, there is an added imperative to detect carefully how to apply the principles I have outlined so far.

As a final summary, in the next chapter I shall look at the application of the principles within the curriculum.

Notes

1   In general, absolute behaviourism has lost ground in current psychology although programmes for enhancing positive behaviour include aspects of modification in the ways outlined here. What is true is that any behaviour, and the consequences directly experienced in connection with it, will have an influence upon subsequent conduct. What that influence is, and how it works to modify subsequent conduct, is worth pondering. Especially with pupils whose self-concept is not fully integrated, it needs to be more than a direct matter of pleasure and pain. One alternative approach in psychology is that of Kelly (1963) whose original writing is difficult to read but whose construct theory is well explained elsewhere (for example, Ravenette 1999). It has the advantage, in line with the principles suggested here, of focusing upon experience and how to make use of it in terms of the behaviours that develop. This, in turn, is, as we have seen, dependent on the level of language development; and both these aspects repay fuller study.

Further reading and study

For development of the ideas of Kelly (1963)
Ravenette, T. (1999) *Personal Construct Theory in Educational Psychology: A Practitioner's View.* London: Whurr.

For an extended discussion of the relationship of language and conduct
Beitchman, J. H., Cohen, N. J., Konstantareas, M. M. and Tannock, R. (eds) (1996) *Language, Learning and Behavior Disorders: Developmental, Biological and Clinical Perspectives.* Cambridge: Cambridge University Press.

CHAPTER 7

Endpiece

Summary of the argument

I have tried, in the foregoing pages, to set out the underlying rationale, that is the principles, in accordance with which all aspects of programme planning can be set. The principles reflect normal development which may well be impaired in pupils with difficulties but is not, generally, totally absent. It is of benefit to both pupil and teacher, therefore, to seek to place aspects of each pupil's special educational needs within such a normal framework – seeking an understanding *from the inside outward.*

Language and thought flow in an interwoven hierarchy, each step in development depending on the steps previously taken in order to give ready and successful access to learning. This, in turn, will have depended on more fundamental principles of personality to enable the child to come to the formal learning process with the four key elements in place:

1. A sense of identity – 'I'

2. A sense of curiosity

3. A sense of experiment

4. A means of 'exchange of ideas' – inner language and outward communication.

All these are independent of any particular syndrome with which the pupil may be diagnosed. They apply generally to all pupils with special educational needs but are especially important in considering the education of pupils with the most severe and complex difficulties. Often the difficulties they face have inhibited a full realisation of these four fundamentals of development and, therefore, unless positive moves are made to induce their functioning, the lack will have increased the handicap under which the pupils participate in formal schooling.

The principles suggested as underlying the development of language, thinking and behaviour are, likewise, based on natural stages and common-sense reactions to the circumstances that pupils with severe learning difficulties might present to staff. All these are background to the delivery of the curriculum.

The curriculum

The translation of the principles into the curriculum, therefore, must start with the realisation that no pupil can succeed at any subject unless he or she is given the wherewithal to enable learning to take place. In education, at the present time, the effectiveness of any curriculum is to be judged by outcomes. That might seem obvious: to judge quality by results. In this, however, there is always a danger that it may lead to short-sightedness and a tendency to lay the implied blame for lack of achievement upon the pupils: the 'what can you expect from them?' effect. If the sole judgement about a school is thought to depend on the levels of overall results from an examined curriculum, those pupils with assessed difficulties sometimes do not find a ready welcome. This holds for all aspects of pupils' difficulties but is particularly hard on the pupils with apparently the severest problems to overcome.

If, however, the definition of effectiveness commences with an examination of what were the understandings of the principles that illuminated the teaching process, so structured as to enable the pupils to learn because their individual difficulties were accommodated and understood in developmental terms, then any curricular programme will become effective in respecting and releasing the full potential of each pupil. It is not, I would argue, a matter of modifying the curriculum *per se* so much as enabling any curriculum to be approached on principle!

This does not follow a line of emasculating the core of a subject discipline in an attempt to make it appear relevant to pupils with complex difficulties. There is always the danger in simplification that what remains is not essential knowledge that releases the pupil into thinking within a subject but peripheral matter without any linking concepts. At worst this sets pupils to tasks of no developmental merit, such as colouring in pictures of Roman centurions, without even help with developing within the exercise essential hand–eye controls, on the ground that it is somehow history. At best this leaves the pupil with information about a series of disconnected pictures without grasping any idea as to why they are in the mind.

It would seem to be time to return to curriculum approaches that follow the ideas developed by Wilfred Brennan (1985). His work represents the era immediately prior to the establishment of the English and Welsh National Curriculum and is concerned less with levels of accumulated fact than with what is essential for any one pupil in any subject at any one time in his or her development.

He suggests that there are stages of developing knowledge in pupils and that the responsibility of the curriculum setter is to judge, on behalf of the pupil, at which of these levels to pitch the lesson.

There are three levels which any aspect of any subject can be known. He writes:

> Curriculum is shaped by the selection of content as knowledge which is intrinsically worthwhile and such that will facilitate the procedures, criteria and concepts appropriate to the particular kind of human experience it represents... The aim is that pupils should *think themselves* [my italics] through to positions of understanding, insight and appreciation. (p.65)

That being said, knowledge can be viewed developmentally as consisting of what *must* be learned in any discipline, what *should* be learned and, for those who are able to absorb the previous two, finally what *could* be learned. The principle of curriculum application is to set down a definition of what is available for learning so that there is the scope for such development to take place. The minimum responsibility for the teacher is to ensure that knowledge is set before each pupil at the level of *must*: that is, to enable the pupil to grasp what is essentially the point of history, geography, sub-disciplines within science, the basis of mathematics, an appreciation of literature, the potentials of language(s) and to have some appreciation of aesthetics. The outcome of any curricular assessment ought to be, first, whether such essentials have been grasped and, second, how far the pupil has been able to think with such basic knowledge. The principles in this book, applying as they do to the process of thinking, are set out to underpin this view of the curriculum.

The thinking process itself, following Brennan (1985), may also be subdivided profitably into aspects of the knowledge that defines it and the skill that enables it to function.

He lists two parallel approaches: knowledge at a level of *awareness* and next a level of *familiarity* that defines the minimum skill that enables that awareness to happen; which in turn leads to *proficiency* when the essentials of a subject are grasped and can be worked on by the pupil with a degree of independent thought and *thoroughness* as defining the level of skills required to accomplish it. Such an understanding of the essence of a curriculum provides, in its turn, the basis for assessing outcomes by determining how far each pupil has been enabled to utilise his or her process of thought within the essential subject knowledge set out in the published curricular requirements. The question is not then how many accumulated facts are known but 'how aware of the essences is this pupil?'.

All the principles in this book are predicated on the need to create self-aware pupils. They are all about *awareness*. Without awareness there is no foundation for any progress into real subject knowledge. The essence of science, for example, is not that pupils know the periodic tables, although there comes a point in the development of scientific knowledge (to the point of Brennan's 'could') where it is important; but rather that they realise that scientific method is to test hypotheses. As has been argued in this book, an essential principle of exploration is involved and unless it is cultivated first, no science lesson, whatever the result on a performance test, will have fulfilled a basic curricular need. It is necessary to judge an outcome for a pupil in severe difficulties with learning against the question, 'Out of what is it coming?'.

Here is a cameo to illustrate how this can be done. I was standing watching a pupil with severe difficulties in an ordinary, inclusive primary school in a deprived area of a big city. She was playing in the water and sand trays set up for her on the patio immediately outside the classroom. With her, partly as company, partly to help her to play and partly, doubtless, to keep an eye on her so that she did not harm herself, was a lad of average academic competence. He could be said, I suppose, to be missing his geography lesson but what developed was a clear illustration of the imparting of essential knowledge on the one hand and proficiency on the other. In line with the principal principles, he clearly had a grasp of his own identity as having a responsibility towards the other pupil, he clearly demonstrated a grasp of experimentation and he had managed to establish communication with the girl, even though she had little speech. He coaxed her into building up piles of sand and then letting water run down from the top – which she enjoyed. Then came the essential difference between occupation and learning. He drew attention to what the water was doing: making channels in the sand. Different piles, different quantities of water, different patterns in the sand. He was a geographer observing land formations but he was using commentary to draw her attention to what she was doing; not in geographical terms – the technical language would have been too complex – but at a level of visual awareness that would be a must for future development. As a lesson in both inclusion and curricular outcomes it was fascinating.

As principles are applied and development takes place (including instruction from the more knowledgeable) so pupils can be guided through Brennan's stages as necessary. It can be argued that it is better to have awareness of many essential aspects of a subject than it is to have a series of facts but without the connectivity to relate them one to the other.

The application of the principles to the curriculum, therefore, is one of enablement and penetration. Penetration because they show the way into such essential knowledge of curriculum subjects; enablement in that they respect the integrity of each pupil and offer an *inside-out* approach to activating the potential for acquiring such knowledge.

Progress in grammatical development: key markers

With pupils with apparent lack of speech or with apparent limited language application, the teacher *as detective* faces a dilemma. By listening and noting what language the pupil uses the teacher can more or less place him or her within the sequence of development shown below. However, the pupil is likely to be older in years than children usually are when these stages evolve and so it may be that he or she has a brain capacity (growth) for inner-language development more developed than is apparent in the outward speech.

Nevertheless, it would be foolish not to confirm that development stages are in place before requiring the pupil to respond with any understanding of what is going on around him or her in the classroom. By listening critically to the use a pupil makes of language in speech and noting to what he or she responds in the language of the adults around, the observer-detective can form a fairly reliable impression of how much linguistic competence the pupil has developed.

This gives a baseline for the use of language programmes to enable pupils to grow into learning effectively. If language used *to* the pupil is too much in advance of this baseline then the poor performance of the pupil is not a matter of low intellect so much as bad programming. Similarly, if the programme as taught neglects the consecutive stages of the key markers (below), skipping stages or not allowing experience of each stage to be embedded in the pupil's mind before moving on, then it will equip that pupil with inadequate tools for learning and the outcomes will not satisfy anyone, least of all the pupil.

In suggesting these key features I have followed Crystal, Fletcher and Garman (1976) but the selection of key features for observation is my own and not to be laid at their door(s).

Table A1 Steps in the development of grammar	
Observed language behaviour	**Detectable feature**
Single-word utterance	Focus words – may be noun or verb but can be extended grammatically by adult in the immediate context, e.g. 'Dada'. 'Yes, you can hear Dada.'; or, 'Gone.' 'Yes, Nana's gone.'
Intonation questions	Voice uses words with tonal variation
Two-word utterances	Structure = subject/verb or subject/complement (without 'is')
	Words may be combined into short phrases, either adject/noun or verb/verb – i.e. two actions with 'assumed' same subject
	Question words begin to be used: 'what X?'
	Verb begins to be used with suffix 'ing' and nouns begin to acquire plural forms (regular)
	Negative: 'No X' (noun or verb)
Three-word utterances	Basic grammatical form of a sentence is established:
	Subject (noun), verb (with tense forms -ing and -ed) – object (noun) or adverb
	Question forms begin to incorporate verb element: 'What X doing?'
	(*Note:* why/because not yet used – the structure needs more than three words to make sense of either the question or the answer)
	Pronominal use begins and third person of verb more common
	Use of preposition/noun
	Adjective/adjective + noun may be heard
	'is' used as the verb element in subject/verb/X (= noun or adjective)

Sentences lengthen to four elements and may use phrases in place of single words within sentence structures, e.g. subject = adjective/noun= 'blue car'	More scope in the sentence construction: subject/verb/(object = adjective/noun) etc. Beginning of use of 'and' within phrases Use of negative within phrases as in: 'That is not an X' Verb extended by simple auxiliary forms and their negatives: *did* do; *have* got; *didn't* do; *haven't* got Time indicated by tenses: 'has happened' or 'will happen', etc. Meaningful use of adverbs (often sounding like adjectives, i.e. without the -*ly* form) Use of 'why' begins as a question form but the answers given to 'why?' questions may not yet be clear or complete until the next stage of development is reached
More complex and therefore more explanatory language is reached – both expressively and receptively At this point and with increasingly skilful self-adjustments to grammar – such as correct past tense forms and more complex clause-structures of questioning and explanation pupils will be able to cope with the tasks set in 'classroom thinking': provided the language of the staff is presented skilfully and sensitively	Extensions of the basic 'subject/verb/object' construction are heard in any position Clauses are incorporated: that is, a verb appears in two places – the main verb 'slot' and in words that fulfil one of the other functions, e.g. '*The man who is running* has the baton' The use of 'because' is therefore possible: 'He's cross *because* he lost his toy'

References

Astington, J.W. (1994) *The Child's Discovery of Mind.* London: Fontana.

Bartsch, K. and Wellman, H.M. (1995) *Children Talk About the Mind.* Oxford: Oxford University Press.

Bauer P.J. and Mandler, J.M. (1992) 'Putting the horse before the cart: the use of temporal order in recall of events by one-year-old children.' *Developmental Psychology, 28,* 441–52.

Beitchman, J.H., Cohen, N.J., Konstantareas, N.M. and Tannock, R. (eds) (1996) *Language, Learning and Behavior Disorders: Developmental, Biological and Clinical Perspectives.* Cambridge: Cambridge University Press.

Bishop, D.V.M. (1990) *Handedness and Developmental Disorder.* Hove: Lawrence Erlbaum Associates.

Brennan, W.K. (1985) *Curriculum for Special Needs.* Milton Keynes: Open University Press.

Britton, J. (1970) *Language and Learning.* London: Penguin Books.

Bruner, J.S. (1976) 'Nature and uses of immaturity.' In J.S. Bruner, A. Jolly, and K. Sylva (eds) *Play: Its Role in Development and Evolution.* London: Penguin Books.

Bullowa, M. (1979) 'Prelinguistic communication: a field for scientific research.' In M. Bullowa (ed) *Before Speech: The Beginning of Interpersonal Communication.* Cambridge: Cambridge University Press.

Burke, P. and Cigno, K. (1996) *Support for Families: Helping Children with Learning Disabilities.* Aldershot: Avebury.

Butler, Lord (1971) *The Art of the Possible.* London: Hamish Hamilton.

Cassirer, E. (1946) *Language and Myth.* (trans. S. Langer.) New York: Dover Publications.

Chesterton, G.K. (1936) *Autobiography.* London: Hutchinson.

Clark, C., Dyson, A. and Milward, A. (1998) *Theorising Special Education.* London: Routledge.

Cole, M., Gay, J., Glick, J.A. and Sharp, D.W. (1971) *The Cultural Context of Learning and Thinking: An Exploration in Experimental Anthropology.* London: Methuen.

Cooper, L. and Henderson, R. (eds) (1973) *Something Wrong?* London: Arrow.

Crystal, D. (1987) *The Cambridge Encyclopedia of Language.* Cambridge: Cambridge University Press.

Crystal, D. (1998) *Language Play.* London: Penguin.

Crystal, D., Fletcher, P. and Garman, M. (1976) *The Grammatical Analysis of Language Disability.* London: Edward Arnold.

Daniels, H. (ed) (1993) *Charting the Agenda – Educational Activity after Vygotsky.* London: Routledge.

Donaldson, M. (1986) *Children's Minds.* London: Fontana.

Donaldson, M. (1992) *Human Minds: An Exploration.* London: Penguin Books.

Dunn, J. (1986) 'Growing up in a family world: issues in the social development of young children.' In M. Richards and P. Light (eds) *Children of Social Worlds.* Cambridge: Polity Press.

Dunn, J. (1991) 'Understanding Others: Evidence from Naturalistic Studies in Children.' In A. Whiten *Natural Theories of Mind.* Oxford: Blackwell.

Dyer, C. (1991) 'An end to the slow lane: a critique of the term "slow learner" and its lingering usage.' *Support for Learning, 6,* 2, 66–70.

Dyer, C. and Hadden, A.J. (1981) 'Delayed echolalia in autism: some observations on differences within the term.' *Child: Care, Health and Development, 7,* 331–45.

Erikson, E.H. (1978) *Toys and Reasons: Stages in the Ritualization of Experience.* London: Marion Boyars.

Evans, P. (1986) 'The learning process.' In J. Coupe and J. Porter (eds) *The Education of Children With Severe Learning Difficulties.* London: Croom Helm.

Fisher, R. (1990) *Teaching Children to Think.* Hemel Hempstead: Simon & Schuster Education.

Flack, R., Harris, J., Jordan, R. and Wimpory, D. (1996) *The Special Educational Needs of Children With Autism. Unit 3 Communication* Being a unit in the Distance Education Course of the University of Birmingham, Birmingham: University of Birmingham.

Fleming, I. and Kroese, B.S. (eds) (1993) *People With Learning Disability and Severe Challenging Behaviour: New Developments in Service and Therapy.* Manchester: Manchester University Press.

Fletcher, P. and MacWhinney, B. (eds) (1995) *The Handbook of Child Language.* Oxford: Blackwell.

Fodor, J.A. (1994) *The Elm and the Expert: Mentalese and its Semantics.* Cambridge MA: MIT Press.

Foster-Cohen, S.H. (1999) *An Introduction to Child Language Development.* London: Longman.

Freud, A. (1966) *Normality and Pathology in Childhood.* London: Hogarth Press.

Geary, D.C., and Brown, S.C. (1991) 'Cognitive addition: strategy choice and speed-of-processing differences in gifted, normal and mathematically disabled children.' *Developmental Psychology, 27*, 3, 398–406.

Goldbart, J. (1986) 'The development of language and communication.' In J. Coupe and J. Porter (eds) *The Education of Children With Severe Learning Difficulties.* London: Croom Helm.

Gregory, R.L. (1990) *Eye and Brain: The Psychology of Seeing.* (4th edn.) Oxford: Oxford University Press.

Griffin, D. (1978) *Slow Learners: A Break in the Circle.* London: Woburn Press.

Hickmann, M. (1995) 'Discourse organisation and the development of reference to person, space and time.' In P. Fletcher and B. MacWhinney (eds) *The Handbook of Child Language.* Oxford: Blackwell.

Hoekstra, T. and Kooij, J.G. (1988) 'The innateness hypothesis.' In J.A. Hawkins *Explaining Language Universals.* Oxford: Basil Blackwell.

Hurt, J.S. (1988) *Outside the Mainstream: A History of Special Education.* London: B.T. Batsford.

Jordan, R. and Powell, S. (1995) *Understanding and Teaching Children with Autism.* Chichester: Wiley.

The Journal of Philosophy of Education (Journal of the Philosophy of Education Society of Great Britain). Oxford: Blackwell Publishers.

Kanner, L. (1973) 'Irrelevant and metaphorical language.' In L. Kanner (ed) *Early Infantile Autism Childhood Psychosis: Initial Studies and New Insights.* Washington DC: V.H. Winston & Sons.

Kelly, G.A. (1963) *A Theory of Personality: The Psychology of Personal Constructs.* New York: Norton.

Lahey, M. (1988) *Language Disorders and Language Development.* New York: Macmillan.

Laslett, R. (1997) Personal communication. University of Birmingham (discussion).

Leckman, J.F. and Cohen, D.J. (1994) 'Tic disorders.' In M. Rutter, E. Taylor, and L. Hersov (eds) *Child and Adolescent Psychiatry: Modern Approaches.* (3rd edn.) Oxford: Blackwell Science.

Lieberman, P. (1998) *Eve Spoke: Human Language and Human Evolution.* London: Picador.

Locke, J.L. (1993) *The Child's Path to Spoken Language.* Cambridge MA: Harvard University Press.

Mahler, M.S. (1969) *On Human Symbiosis and the Vicissitudes of Individuation.* (vol. 1) London: The Hogarth Press.

McNeill, D. (1970) *The Acquisition of Language: The Study of Developmental Linguistics.* New York: Harper Row.

Meadows, S. (1993) *The Child As Thinker: The Development and Acquisition of Cognition in Childhood.* London: Routledge.

Menn, L. and Stoel-Gammon, C. (1995) 'Phonological development.' In P. Fletcher and B. MacWhinney (eds) *The Handbook of Child Language.* Oxford: Blackwell.

Morris, D., Collett, P., Marsh, P. and O'Shaughnessy, M. (1979) *Gestures Their Origins and Distribution.* London: Jonathan Cape.

Nelson, K. (ed) (1989) *Narratives From the Crib.* Cambridge MA: Harvard University Press.

Nelson, K. (1996) *Language in Cognitive Development: The Emergence of the Mediated Mind.* Cambridge: Cambridge University Press.

Newell, A. (1977) 'On the analysis of human problem solving protocols.' In P.N. Johnson-Laird and P.C. Watson (eds) *Thinking: Readings in Cognitive Science.* Cambridge: Cambridge University Press.

Nmeroff, C.J. and Karoly, P. (1991) 'Operant methods.' In F. Kanfer, and A.P. Coldstein (eds) *Helping People Change.* (4th edn.) New York: Pergamon.

Obler, L.K. and Gjerlow, K. (1999) *Language and the Brain.* Cambridge: Cambridge University Press.

O'Donohoe, N.V. (1985) *Epilepsies of Childhood.* (2nd edn.) London: Butterworth.

Ouvry, C. (1987) *Educating Children With Profound Handicaps.* Kidderminster: British Institute of Mental Handicap.

Parker, T. and Allerton, R. (1962) *The Courage of His Convictions.* London: Hutchinson.

Pearson, A. and Aloysius, C. (1994) *Museums and Children With Learning Difficulties: The Big Foot.* London: Trustees of the British Museum.

Peel, E.A. (1971) *The Nature of Adolescent Judgment.* London: Crosby Lockwood Staples.

Philips, G.M. and Dyer, C. (1977) 'Late onset echolalia in autism and allied disorders.' *British Journal of Disorders of Communication, 12,* 1, 47–59.

Piaget, J. (1959) *The Language and Thought of the Child* (3rd edn.) London: Routledge & Kegan Paul.

Piaget, J. and Inhelder, B. (1969) *The Psychology of the Child.* London: Routledge & Kegan Paul.

Pinker, S. (1994) *The Language Instinct.* London: Penguin.

Pinker, S. and Bloom, P. (1992) 'Natural language natural selection.' In J.H. Barkow, L. Cosmides and J. Toobey (eds) *The Adapted Mind: Evolutionary Psychology and the Generation of Culture.* New York: Oxford University Press.

Pollard, A. (with Filer, A.) (1996) *The Social World of Children's Learning.* London: Cassell.

Prizant, B.M. (1983) 'Echolalia in autism: assessment and intervention.' *Seminars in Speech and Language, 4,* 63–77.

Ravenette, T. (1999) *Personal Construct Theory in Educational Psychology: A Practitioner's View.* London: Whurr.

Rogoff, B. (1990) *Apprenticeship in Thinking*. New York: Oxford University Press.

Rondal, J.A. and Edwards, S. (1997) *Language in Mental Retardation*. London: Whurr.

Rosetti, L.M. (1996) *Communication Intervention: Birth to Three*. San Diego: Singular.

Schaffer, H.R. (ed) (1977) *Studies in Mother–Infant Interaction*. London: Academic Press.

Scherer, M., Gersch, I. and Fry, L. (eds) (1990) *Meeting Disruptive Behaviour: Assessment, Intervention and Partnership*. Basingstoke: Macmillan Education.

Sheridan, M.D. (1975) *Children's Developmental Progress: From Birth to Five Years: The Stycar Sequences*. (3rd edn.) London: Routledge.

Sheridan, M.D. (1977) *Spontaneous Play in Early Childhood*. Windsor: NFER.

Shotter, J. (1978) 'The cultural context of communication studies: theoretical and methodological issues.' In A. Lock (ed) *Action, Gesture and Symbol: The Emergence of Language*. London: Academic Press.

Siegler, R.S. (1996) *Emerging Minds: The Process of Change in Children's Thinking*. New York: Oxford University Press.

Skinner, B.F. (1972) 'Compassion and ethics in the care of the retardate.' In B.F. Skinner (ed) *Cumulative Record*. Washington DC: Joseph P. Kennedy Foundation of Mental Retardation.

Stern, D. (1977) *The First Relationship: Infant and Mother*. London: Open Books.

Sugden, D. (ed) (1989) *Cognitive Approaches in Special Education*. Lewes: The Falmer Press.

Talay-Ongan, A. (1998) *Typical and Atypical Development in Early Childhood: The Fundamentals*. Leicester: The British Psychological Society.

Tansley, A.E. and Gulliford, R. (1960) *The Education of Slow Learning Children*. London: Routledge & Kegan Paul.

Tighe, T.J., and Leaton, R.N. (eds) (1976) *Habituation: Perspectives from Child Development, Animal Behaviour and Neurophysiology*. Hillsdale NJ: Lawrence Erlbaum Associates.

Tizard, B. (1985) 'Social relationships between adults and young children and their impact in intellectual functioning.' In R.A. Hinde, A.N. Perry-Clermont and J. Stevenson-Hinde *Social Relationships and Cognitive Development*. (Symposium of the Fyssen Foundation.) Oxford: The Clarendon Press.

Toobey, J. and Cosmides, L. (1992) 'The psychological foundations of culture.' In J.H. Barkow, L. Cosmides and J. Toobey *The Adapted Mind: Evolutionary Psychology and the Generation of Culture*. New York: Oxford University Press.

Vygotsky, L.S. (1962) *Thought and Language*. Cambridge MA: MIT Press.

Warnock, M. (1998) *An Intelligent Person's Guide to Ethics*. London: Duckworth.

Waterhouse, S. (2000) *A Positive Approach to Autism*. London: Jessica Kingsley Publishers.

Weir, R. (1962) *Language in the Crib*. The Hague: Mouton.

Wellman, H.M. (1990) *The Child's Theory of Mind.* Cambridge MA: MIT Press.

Wells, G. (1986) *The Meaning Makers: Children Learning Language and Using Language to Learn.* London: Hodder and Stoughton.

Whiten, A. (ed) (1991) *Natural Theories of Mind: Evolution, Development and Simulation of Everyday Mindreading.* Oxford: Blackwell.

Wierzbicka, A. (1996) *Semantics: Primes and Universals.* Oxford: Oxford University Press.

Williams, D. (1996) *Autism: An Inside-Out Approach.* London: Jessica Kingsley Publishers.

Williams, P. (1970) 'Slow-learning children and educational problems.' In P. Mittler (ed) *The Psychological Assessment of Mental and Physical Handicap.* London: Methuen.

Wood, D. (1986) 'Aspects of teaching and learning.' In M. Richards and P. Light (eds) *Children of Social Worlds.* Cambridge: Polity Press.

Wood, D. (1998) *How Children Think and Learn.* 2nd edn. Oxford: Blackwell.

Zimmer, D.E. (1986) *So Kommt Der Mensch Zur Sprache.* Zurich: Haffmans Verlag.

Subject Index

achievement 39
actor
    child in learning process 94
actuality 96–7, 119–123.
    see also possibility
adolescence 149–51, 158
age
    as a concept 145
analysis
    see under problem analysis
answer
    knowing the answer first 77
    teaching the answer first 111
antecedents
    of actions 88, 133
    of behaviours 53
Ashaninca language 117
attention
    paying 25, 97–8, 108–9
    seeking 140–1
auditory field
    guidance for pupils 108–9
autism
    autistic spectrum disorder 35n, 45,
        55, 69, 90
awareness 170
awkwardness 51–2

'because'
    importance of 65, 86–9, 103,
        140–3, 162
behaviour 15, 52–3, 67, 87, 122,
    appeasement 154–55
    appropriate 124, 142–151
    challenging 131–2, 138, 161–3
    positive approaches to 15, 135–142
behaviour modification 99, 129, 166n
biting 45–8, 134
    self 160–61
blame 152–57
body language 34, 41, 48, 90, 164

brain 65–72
    age 145
    damage 64
    development 59–60
    freeze 122
    impairment 152
    information to 42
    injury to 83
    instinct 46
    organisation 20, 28
    processing 138
    sense co-ordination 50–1, 106–7
    social interaction 90
    thinking 94–9
British Museum 78

Channel tunnel 12
choice 105–6, 136–7
    different from selection 105–6
clues 37–55
    for teachers 13–14, 89,
    for pupils re. connectivity 121
    from touch and taste 109
classroom 11, 33, 82, 111, 114, 126,
    156
code 128–9
conversation 87
    control 91
    culture 148
    language in 64, 65, 116
    management 34, 92n, 147
    observation 38, 40
    space for pupils 136
code 127–136, 140, 152, 155, 158
    agreed among staff 165
    culture 144
    for handling extreme behaviour
        158–161
    social 143–7
cognitive
    capability 157
    capacity 163
    development 103
    processes 76
    skills 95

Comenius
    see KomenskýFD
commentary 23–6, 29, 61, 68, 116, 171
    inner 71
communication 20, 66, 72, 81–2, 90–2,
    167
    alternative 34
    as behaviour 58
    behaviour as 131
    boards 64, 87–8
    curiosity 28
    different from language 33, 59
    difficulty 31
    fun 33
    intent 34
    non-vocal 34–5
    systems 33, 136
contemplation 31, 123n, 136
control 34, 136–8, 142
conversation(s) 84–5
coprolalia 86
curiosity 19, 27–31, 85, 110, 167
curriculum 15, 18, 168–171
    application 114
    planning 11
Czech Republic 9, 14

Darwin, Charles 93n
daydream 42–3
detective
    stories 13, 15,
work for staff 22, 72, 83–4, 90, 97–8,
    101, 136, 153, 163
development(al)
    appropriate to age 144–7
    'blips' 68
    in puberty 150
    infant language 73
    lack 114
    levels 110, 113
    processes 27
    sequences 56n, 64, 67
    stages 22, 113, 145
dialogue 24, 28, 69, 75, 78, 83, 94,
    123n, 149

    lack of 134
    with ourselves 80
disability awareness 19
discourse 113–15, 122, 152

ear(s) 45, 48–50, 98
echolalia 69–72
    delayed 71–2
    immediate 69–71
education 31, 67, 114, 123n, 164, 168
    basic question in 9–10, 17n
    need in puberty 150
        objective 128
        practice 9, 105
    process 28, 35, 36n
    progress 137
educator 73, 104
    role of 15, 39, 115
ego 21
egocentric 21
emotional state of child 62
epilepsy 152
    epileptiform activity 43, 83
ethics 127
exclusion 130
experience 11, 19, 28, 54, 63, 67–8,
    77–8, 84, 100
    definition 12–13
    range of 34
experiment 19, 27–31, 75, 81, 85,
    101–4, 110, 164, 167
    scientific 30
exploration 111, 170
eye(s) 41–5, 51, 98
    contact 25–6, 41, 44

figure-ground 107
finger pointing 29
foundations
    of education 10–11
fun 32, 36n, 81–2, 85, 91

gaze 42–4
gossip 91

grammar 60, 62–3, 67, 92n, 172–4
grin 45, 48

habituation 50
handedness 50
    see also hemispheric dominance
handicap 18–19, 28
hemispheric dominance
    in brain 51, 56n
home language 60
    contrast with foreign 62

'I' (first person pronoun)
    instruction in use of 21–2
    pupils' use of 22–31, 93n
id 21
idea(s) 19, 101
idiolect 81, 92n
identity 19, 20–6, 32, 34–5, 35n, 89,
    167
    linguistic 23
    interaction with mother 24
individual education plan (IEP) 11
imagination 13, 39, 139, 162
inclusion 9
    inclusive classes 114, 130, 133,
        170–1
individuation 20
information technology [IT] 78
inner language 23, 59, 79–91, 157–8,
    167
    see also inner speech
    use in planning 152
inner speech 23, 25–6, 30, 33, 96,
    79–83, 101, 113, 116, 162, 164
    first report in 125
    intention in 141
    process of 84
inside out
    definition 13–14, 35n
    helping in behaviour 125
    theory of mind 162
    understanding 19, 38, 146–7, 152
    working from 104, 133, 171

IQ 64, 94–5, 104, 119, 145
intention 83, 86–8, 90, 125, 141,
    152–7, 161–5
interaction
    infant-mother 21, 35n, 66
    interactional communication 27

jokes 33, 85

key words 109
knowledge 169
Komensk̈yFD, Jan Amos 17n
Kpelle
    people of Liberia 112

language 14, 20, 39,
    development 58–9, 61, 74, 79,
        84, 91–2, 156
    identity 23
        instinct 59–69
        instructional 23, 62, 138
        interplay 32
        motherese 61, 63
        not same as communication 33,
            58–9
        pre-sleep soliloquy 88
        social context 73, 75–6, 111,
            133
        thinking and l. 115–123, 167
        tone and rhythm 90
learning 29, 53, 101
    at mother's knee 18
    social 20, 31, 35n
learning style 37
lesson(s)
    planning 39
    stimulus in 107
libido 21
listening
    for a key-word 29, 109
    skill in language and thinking 49
London 107, 112

masturbation 150–1
meaning 12, 42, 46, 70, 73, 81, 115,
    117
    confusion 49
    contextual 118
    cultural 112
    echolalic phrases 72
    inner 80
    instinct for 92
    need to define 118
    semantics 59, 73, 92n
    transference 33
memory 29, 97, 98–102, 120–2, 123n
    motor- 99, 103, 107, 138
mental age 145
    confusion in use 151
mental pain 44
metaphor 59, 74, 76, 82, 92n, 95, 98,
    112
mind 27, 43, 68, 89, 92, 106, 113,
    116,120, 123n, 125, 152, 169
    active 12
    adult 155–7
    awareness of own m. 21
concept of 66, 146
    language in 82
    loss of balance in 122
skills in 118
Monet 117
morality 113
Moravia 9
motherese
    see under language
mouth 45–8

Newham, London Borough of 9
normality 15
number
    stories in teaching 75–8

observation 37, 40–53, 97–8, 162
    in classroom 114
obsessions 101
one-to-one

caution concerning 137
outcome(s)
    for pupils 10, 97, 100, 165,
        168–71
    of observation 55–6

panic 115, 122, 159–60, 162
parent(s) 53–4, 56n, 102, 126, 130, 158
participant language 123n
perception 29, 95
    self-perception. 35n
philosophy 10, 17n, 113
physical difficulty 137
physical handling
    notes in guidance for 158–161
play 30–1, 75, 80, 119, 156, 162, 170
    a play 112
    with hand-puppets 91
poetry 33
possibility 96–7, 119–123
posture 51
principles
    definition 16n, 167
problem analysis
    of behaviour 125–132, 148, 154,
        157
problem solving
    by pupils 106–7
programme(s) 10, 28, 76, 91, 104–5,
    107, 110, 139, 142, 166n
    based on reason 10, 17n
    planning 167
prompt
    in echolalia 70
psychology 94, 101, 166n
psychologist(s) 38, 145, 153
    reports from 109
psychometric tests 14, 101, 104, 109
    see also IQ
punishment 127–30, 152
    confused with management 130

reasoning 74, 126, 142, 164
record sheets

for behaviours 136
running away 24

'say to yourself'
    technique in lessons 23, 29, 34, 116
schema(s) 82, 95
self
    awareness 66–7
    control 35, 140–2, 160, 165
    in social context 32
    sense of 21, 23, 26, 87, 150, 164
semantics
    see under meaning
senses 28–9
sexual development 146–151
'slow learners'
    phrase rejected 95
sign system(s) 87, 131, 137
smell
    see taste
social context 75–6, 85, 96, 99, 111–15,
    126
social conventions 15
    acceptability within 101
    conditioning by 127
    expectations within 148–151
social interactions 60,81, 90, 136
    emotional reactions within 134–6
    dialogue within 64, 91
society 18, 20, 127–8
space 24, 136–8
spectator language 123n
speculation 96–7, 100–1, 97, 115
speech 31, 33–4, 45, 61–2, 79, 83, 90
staff training
    re. challenging behaviour 135
story(ies) 32, 73–4, 78, 92n, 117
syntax
    see also grammar
    organisational role 65, 140, 165
    patterns 60, 89

taste 45–6, 109–11
task(s) 102–4, 142

Theory of Mind 21, 48, 113–5, 123n,
    155, 162
thinking 14, 39, 82, 163–6, 169
    development 117–18
    'think!' as command 118
    t. about thinking 119–123
thought process 13, 59, 73, 82–3, 86,
    167
    generation 102–3
    formed by language 90
    'second thought mode' 135
thumb-sucking 47, 146–9
touch 109–111
time 138–140
    continuous 120
Tourette syndrome 86

videotaping 123n, 153–4
visual field
    guidance needed 108–9
vocabulary 30, 33

'why' questions
    see under 'because'
word 64, 73–4
    counts 83
    lists 91
    one w. stage 67–8
    three w, stage 73

Author Index

Allerton, R. 129
Aloysious, C. 78
Astington, J.W. 156

Bartasch, K. 146
Bauer, P.J. 60
Beitchman, J.H. 124, 166
Bentley, E.C. 37, 55
Bishop, D.V.M. 51, 56, 57
Bloom, P. 59
Brennan, W.K. 169, 170, 171
Britton, J. 123
Brown, S.C. 95
Browning, R. 94
Bruner, J.S. 27
Bullowa, M. 60
Burke, P. 56, 57
Butler, R.A. 94

Cassirer, E. 73, 92
Chesterton, G.K. 38, 74
Cigno, K. 56, 57
Clark, C. 17
Cohen, D.J. 86, 166
Cole, M. 112
Cooper, L. 19, 20
Cosmides, L. 60, 94, 95
Crystal, D. 36, 60, 61, 68, 92, 93, 173

Daniels, H. 79
Donaldson, M. 65, 96
Doyle, A.C. 39.56
Dunn, J. 113, 143
Dyer, C. 70, 72, 95
Dyson, A. 17

Edwards, S. 152
Erikson, E.H. 27

Evans, P. 98

Filer, A. 36
Fisher, R.123
Flack, R. 91
Fletc her, P. 60, 68, 92, 93, 173
Fleming, I. 131
Fodor, J.A. 120
Foster-Cohen, S.H. 93
Freud, A. 21
Fry, L. 129

Garman, M. 60, 68, 92, 93, 173
Geary, D.C. 95
Gersch, I. 129
Gjerlow, K. 66,99
Golbart, J. 58
Gregory, R.L. 43
Griffin, D. 95
Gulliford, R. 95

Hadden, A.J. 72
Henderson, R. 19,20
Hickmann, M. 113
Hoekstra, T. 60
Hurt, J.S. 148

Inhelder, B. 21

Jordan, R. 36

Kanner, L. 72
Karoly, P. 99
Keatinge, M.W. 17
Kelly, G.A. 166
KomenskÿFD, J.A. 17
Konstantareas, M.M. 166
Kooij, J.G. 60
Kroese, B.S. 131

Lahey, M. 58
Laslett, R. 126
Leaton, R.N. 50
Leckman, J.F. 86
Lieberman, P. 90, 93, 94
Locke, J.L. 59

Mahler, M.S. 20
Mandler, J.M. 60
McNeill, D. 63
Meadows, S. 77, 97, 98, 112, 119, 123
Menn, L. 81
Milward, A. 17
Morris, D. 41

Nelson, K. 14, 80, 81, 88, 123
Newell, A. 106
Nmeroff, C.J. 99

Obler, L.K. 66, 99
O'Donohoe, N.V. 43, 152
Ouvry, C. 98

Parker, T. 129
Pearson, A. 78
Peel, E.A. 79
Philips, G.M. 70
Piaget, J. 21, 80, 81, 82
Pinker, S. 14, 59
Pollard, A. 36
Powell, S. 36
Prizant, B.H. 72

Ravenette, T. 166
Rogoff, B. 36
Rondal, J.A. 152
Rosetti, L.M. 58

Schaffer, H.R. 35, 36, 60, 80
Scherer, M. 129
Sheridan, M.D. 27, 56, 57, 145

Shotter, J. 103
Siegler, R.S. 74, 106
Skinner, B.F. 129
Stern, D. 60
Stoel-Gammon, C. 81
Sugden, D. 165

Talay-Ongan, A. 56, 57
Tannnock, R. 166
Tansley, A.E. 95
Tighe, T.J. 50
Tizard, B. 18
Toobey, J. 60, 94, 95

Vygotsky, L.S. 79, 80, 81, 82

Warnock, M. 127
Waterhouse, S. 101
Weir, R. 80, 81, 88
Wellman, H.M. 21, 79, 113, 146
Wells, G. 32
Whiten, A. 21, 66, 113
Wierzbicka, A. 93
Williams, D. 35, 36
Williams, P. 95
Wood, D. 112, 123

Zimmer, D.E. 60

Index to Principles

behaviour 124–5
  first 125
    implications for teaching 132
  second 142
    implications for teaching 147
  third 152
    implications for teaching 157
  fourth 161
    implications for teaching 163

language 59
  first 59
    implications for teaching 61
  second 65
    implications for teaching 67
  third 73
    implications for teaching 74
  fourth 79
  fifth 81
    implications for teaching 82
  sixth
    implications for teaching 16

principal 19
  first 20
    implications for teaching 21
  second and third 27
    implications for teaching 28
  fourth 31
    implications for teaching 33

thinking 96
  first 96
    implications for teaching 102
  second 105
    implications for teaching 107
  third 111
    implications for teaching 113
  fourth 115
    implications for teaching
  fifth 119
    implications for teaching 121